Key Stage 2 English Spelling & Vocabulary

WORKBOOK 2

Foundation Level

Dr Stephen C Curran
with Warren Vokes
Edited by Mark Schofield

This book belongs to

Accelerated Education Publications Ltd

found	count	hall
mouth	rain	train
again	find	kind
wind	home	nose

Exercise 24a

1) It was __raining__ heavily so we sheltered under a tree.

2) The maid opened the front door and showed the gentleman into the _____ .

3) I taught my younger brother to _____ from one to ten.

4) His _____ took him to school and then she drove to the supermarket.

5) One screw was too long and the _____ was too short.

6) She had caught a cold and her _____ was blocked and sore.

7) As he was _____ along the road he saw his friend coming towards him.

8) _____ Malone was writing his sermon for next Sunday.

9) The doctor looked in his _____ and could see that his throat was very red.

10) I paid for my _____ ticket at the station booking office.

Score /10

Exercise 24b

11) He was _____ his best to stay calm but he was very excited.

12) He gave her a single red _____ on their wedding anniversary.

13) "Can you help me _____ my ring? I dropped it over here."

14) We _____ it under the armchair.

15) It snowed on Monday and Tuesday and _____ on Saturday.

16) I stayed at _____ to watch the football match on television.

17) She went to the circus with her older _____ and his friends.

18) So strong was the _____ that it blew the tiles off the roof.

19) The driver was very _____ and helped the old lady off the bus.

20) The use of hosepipes was banned due to the lack of _____ .

Score /10

© 2005 Stephen Curran

Word Bank

rose, doing, other, brother, going, raining, mother, father

TOTAL 480

Across

3. Releasing water from the sky.
5. To discover something.
6. Water falling from clouds.
8. Say numbers in order.
10. Air moving fast enough to be noticed.
12. Part of the face used for breathing and smelling.
13. Additional or different from.
15. Prickly shrub with ornamental flowers.
16. A number of railway carriages linked together.
18. Act of leaving somewhere.
19. Female parent.

Down

1. Showing courtesy or caring about somebody.
2. Repeating what has happened before.
4. A male with the same parents as another person.
5. Male parent.
7. Place where a person lives.
9. Past tense of find.
11. Act of carrying out something.
14. Entrance room.
17. Opening in the head where food goes in and sound comes out.

24

Put the mystery letter from the starred square (✱) into the box marked **24** below. Add in the mystery letters from puzzles **25** to **31** then rearrange them to make **Dickens's Mystery Word**.

The clue is **SPORT**.

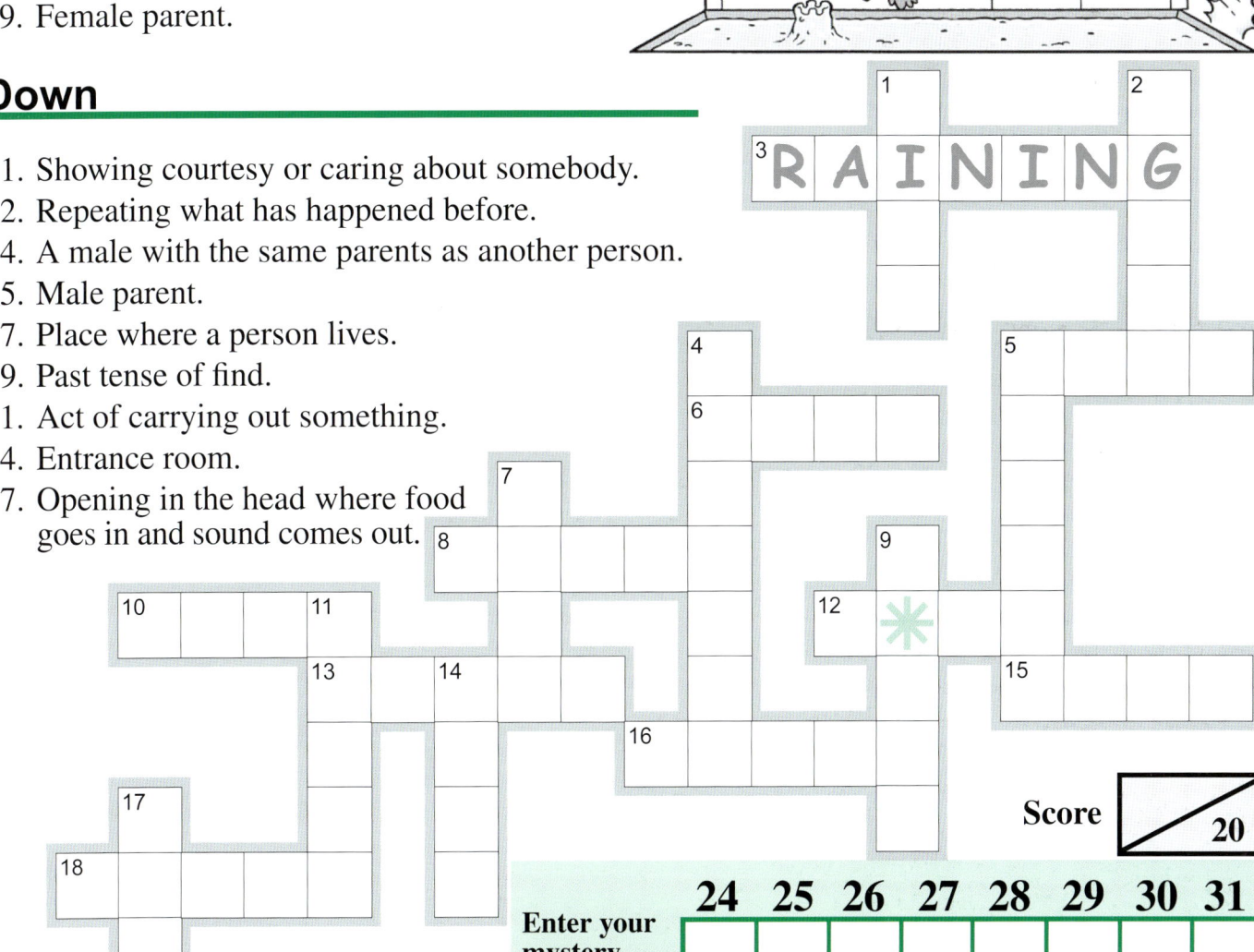

Score ⬚ / 20

24 25 26 27 28 29 30 31

Enter your mystery letters here:

Now rearrange them to make the:

Mystery Word:

© 2005 Stephen Curran

winter   summer   ate
late   gate   sister
able   table   dinner
supper   butter   back

Across

1. In a position to do something.
3. Liquid occurring as rain, snow and ice.
5. Travel through the air.
6. A female with the same parents as another person.
8. The part at the rear of something.
9. Not wet.
12. A piece of furniture with a flat top and one or more legs.
14. Between spring and autumn.
15. Affected by an illness.
16. Happening or arriving after the expected time.
17. Main meal of the day.

Down

2. Soft creamy spread made by churning cream.
3. Between autumn and spring.
4. The darkest colour, completely dark with no light.
6. Evening meal.
7. Hinged barrier that closes a gap in a wall or fence.
10. Past tense of eat.
11. Common water bird.
13. Amount of money owed.
15. The number 7.

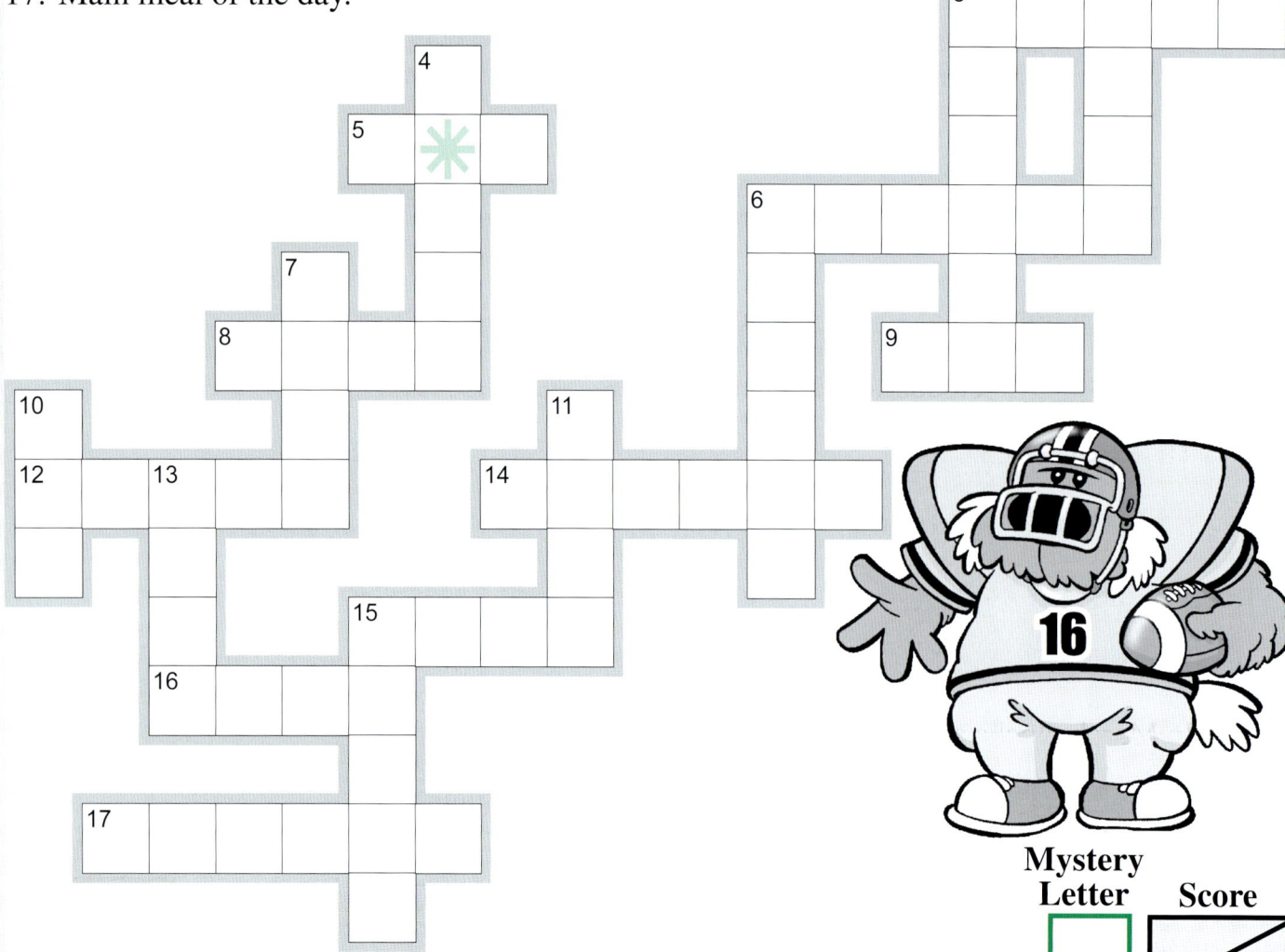

Mystery Letter

Score 20

© 2005 Stephen Curran

black **sick**
fly **dry**
seven **water**
bill **duck**

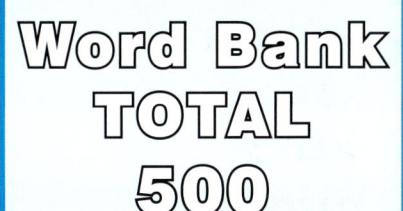

Exercise 25a

1) By standing on the stool he was _____ to reach the top shelf.

2) He was so tall that he had to _____ his head to go through the doorway.

3) The nurse gave Stephanie a glass of _____ and told her to drink it slowly.

4) The notice in reception said that _____ would be served from 7.30 to 9.00pm.

5) Why do some birds _____ south for the winter?

6) Because he had overslept that morning he was very _____ for work.

7) She gave her friend three of the ten sweets but kept _____ for herself!

8) She told him he should not have so much _____ on his toast.

9) In the _____ some birds migrate to a warmer country.

10) The soil was so _____ that nothing would grow there.

Score /10

Exercise 25b

11) We had a light _____ later in the evening.

12) _____ clouds were gathering and it looked like rain.

13) The telephone _____ was much higher than last month.

14) He _____ only a little celery but really enjoyed the cheese.

15) The old kitchen _____ needed to be stripped and revarnished.

16) The crowd were asked to move _____ to allow the ambulance through.

17) In March clocks are put forward one hour for British _____ Time.

18) The latch and hinges on the _____ needed oiling.

19) She had eaten too much chocolate and felt very _____ .

20) Your mother's _____ is your aunt.

Score /10

© 2005 Stephen Curran

snow	blow	grow
kitten	letter	lesson
sorry	funny	sunny
little	show	happy

Exercise 26a

1) The house lights dimmed, the curtains opened and the _____ began.

2) The little _____ was lost and was crying for her mummy.

3) The policeman took her _____ and led her away from the danger.

4) I _____ to visit my grandparents on Sunday afternoons.

5) He went to the airfield for his first flying _____ .

6) When asked if he was enjoying the day he said he was really _____ .

7) The _____ had climbed the tree and could not get back down.

8) I wrote a long _____ to my pen friend in Germany.

9) It was so _____ during the power cut we had to light a candle.

10) When I _____ up I want to be a scientist.

Score /10

Exercise 26b

11) The _____ time I went ice skating I kept falling down.

12) They could not wait to play in the _____ with their new sledge.

13) While on holiday in Greece it was really _____ for most of the time.

14) The spelling test was very _____ and I did not do very well.

15) My dad was in bed with the flu and felt very _____ for himself.

16) The joke was very _____ and they all laughed.

17) He was told that _____ day he could go on the bus by himself.

18) On television they showed the vet treating a _____ with a broken wing.

19) There was _____ chance of my team winning the game.

20) "Be careful, it's hot! _____ on it to cool it down."

Score /10

© 2005 Stephen Curran

Word Bank

arm
dark
bird
one
hard
girl
first
love

Word Bank TOTAL 520

26

Across

1. Female child.
4. Upper limb attached to the shoulder.
6. Message sent by post.
7. Young cat.
8. To like very much.
9. Feeling pleasure, contentment or joy.
12. Two-legged with wings, beak and feathers.
15. A single thing or unit.
16. To make something visible or to point something out.
17. Frozen water that falls to the ground as ice crystal flakes.
18. Feeling or expressing regret.

Down

2. Small or of less than average size.
3. Not light or lit.
5. Causing amusement or laughter.
9. Firm, stiff, or rigid and not easily cut pierced, or bent.
10. Before the rest.
11. To develop and become larger in size.
12. To move something with a current of air.
13. Period of time spent teaching or learning.
14. With a lot of sunshine.

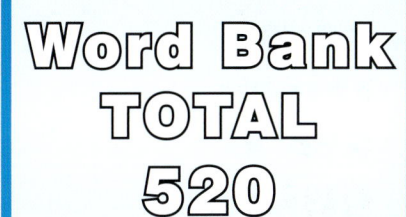

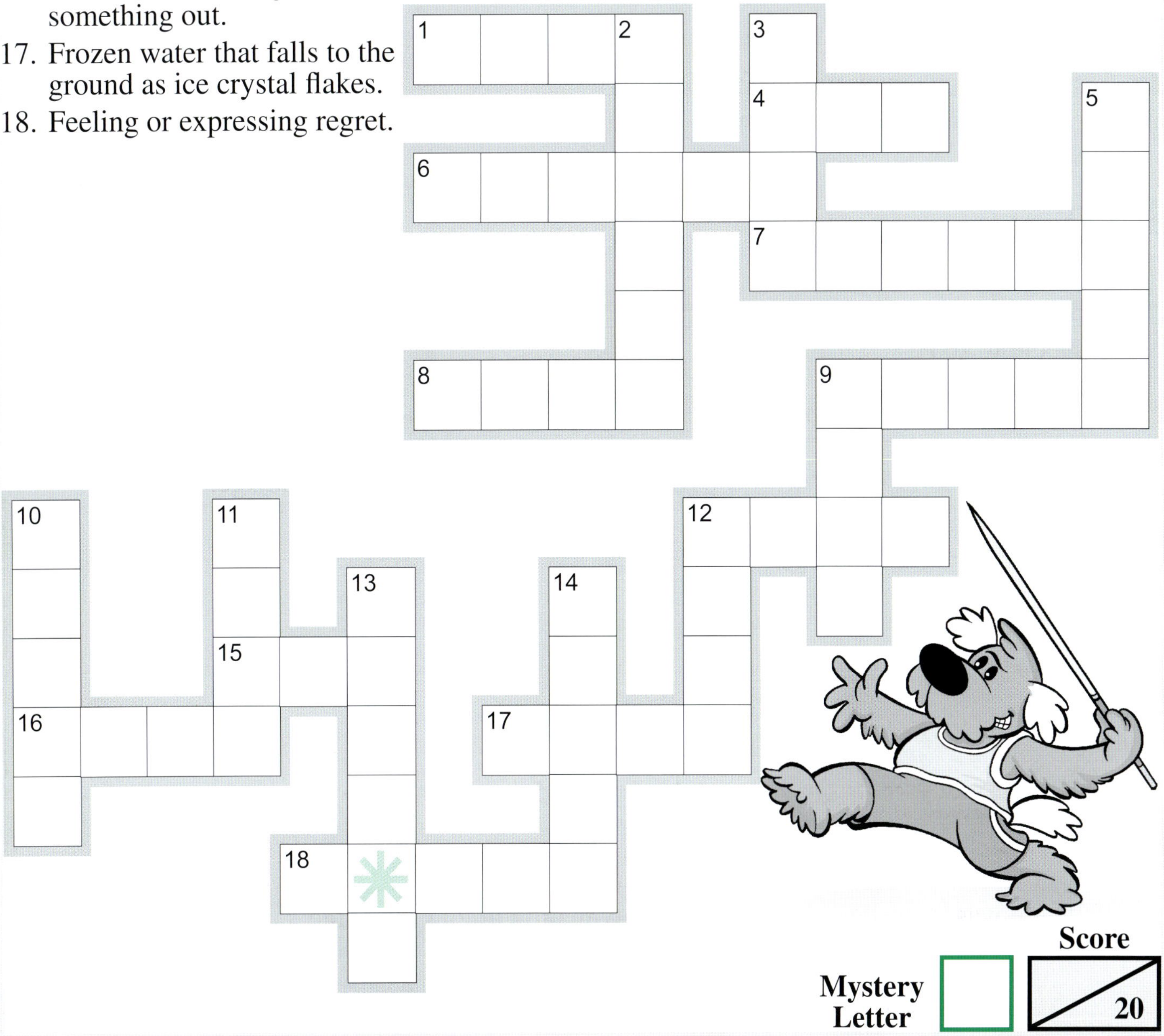

Mystery Letter

Score 20

© 2005 Stephen Curran

come coming making
river spoke smoke
fire hair chair
fair pretty dress

27

Across

2. Reasonable and unbiased, according to the rules.
3. Every one.
6. Creative activity.
7. Very young child.
10. Strands growing on the head or body.
11. Narrow-leaved plant that grows in fields and gardens.
13. Most recent or after all the others.
15. To put on clothes.
18. Exchanged for money.
19. Large natural channel of fresh water.
20. To arrive, reach, or originate from.

Down

1. Having a pleasant face.
4. Happening soon.
5. Small, imaginary supernatural creature with magic powers.
8. Seat with a back and sometimes with an armrest.
9. Moving quickly.

Down (continued)

12. Cloud of tiny particles in the air from something burning.
14. An account of an event.
16. One of a set of bars or rods from the hub that supports the rim of a wheel.
17. A pile of burning fuel.

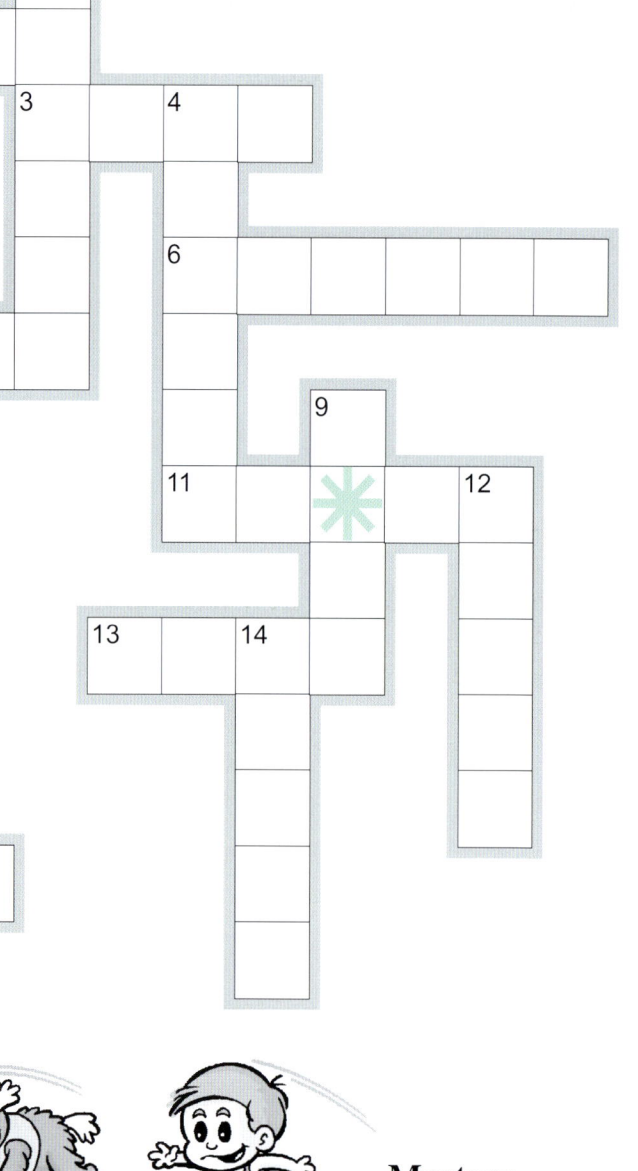

Mystery Letter

Score

20

Word Bank

grass   baby
story   fairy
fast   last
each   sold

TOTAL 540

Exercise 27a

1) She read him a _____ before he went to sleep.

2) The barber cut his _____ really short.

3) Her _____ was hungry and was crying loudly.

4) They are £3.00 _____ so I can buy four for £12.00.

5) The recent rainfall had made the _____ swollen and fast flowing.

6) The baker's shop had _____ every loaf of bread by four o'clock.

7) "Thomas! _____ here at once!" said the teacher.

8) The _____ was thick and the firemen could not see very well.

9) She _____ very softly so as not to frighten the animal.

10) Sitting by the roaring _____ he soon became much warmer.

Score /10

Exercise 27b

11) The early morning dew had made the _____ too damp to sit on.

12) The blue car was _____ but the green one was faster.

13) He sat on a _____ by the window looking at the birds in the garden.

14) He caught the _____ bus home which left at 11.30pm.

15) His car was _____ a strange noise and he pulled onto the hard shoulder.

16) "I'm _____ ! Wait for me!"

17) She made a _____ to decorate the top of the Christmas tree.

18) It was a deep cut and the nurse used a large bandage to _____ the wound.

19) The village had many thatched cottages with _____ gardens.

20) It is very important that they are given a _____ trial.

Score /10

© 2005 Stephen Curran

cold	colder	penny
add	apple	over
only	after	ear
hear	dear	talk

Exercise 28a

1) The night was _____ , frosty and very, very dark.

2) The tractor was parked across the farmyard _____ the barn.

3) The door and window frames of our _____ are painted blue.

4) He could clearly _____ the aircraft approaching the runway.

5) If you need to know the time _____ a policeman.

6) Somehow the prisoner had climbed _____ the wall and escaped.

7) He had bought a new set of stamps to _____ to his collection.

8) They liked to _____ along the bank of the canal and watch the boats go by.

9) She used to ride her _____ through the park every weekend.

10) Last _____ we went to Spain for our holiday.

Score /10

Exercise 28b

11) He wanted four oranges but there were _____ three left.

12) They set a trap for the _____ but they failed to catch it.

13) The day became _____ as the sun went down and the temperature dropped.

14) The new fence was much higher _____ the old one.

15) "A _____ for the guy," the children shouted to passers-by.

16) I went to the library to hear a lady _____ about our local history.

17) His old aunt was very _____ to him and he missed her when she died.

18) Every day he had an _____ with his lunch.

19) The programme was on _____ my bedtime so I recorded it.

20) He put drops in his _____ to soften the wax.

Score /10

© 2005 Stephen Curran

walk horse
house mouse
than year
near ask

Word Bank TOTAL 560

Across 28

4. No more and no less.
5. Small rodent with a long mostly hairless tail.
7. Put something into something else.
9. A position directly above something.
12. Beloved or costly.
14. Compared with.
15. To perceive sounds.
16. A twelve-month period.
17. Not far away but close by.
19. To move or travel on foot.

Down

1. To speak.
2. At or with a low temperature.
3. Cooler still.
6. Organ of hearing and balance.
8. A building made for people to live in.
10. Later than.
11. Small bronze coin used in Britain before 1971.
13. Firm round fruit with a central core.
15. A four-legged animal with a mane, tail, hooves and a long head.
18. To put a question to somebody.

Mystery Letter

Score 20

© 2005 Stephen Curran

face	race	left
eye	eyes	tail
more	store	plant
wait	miss	lady

Across

2. A greater number than before.
5. To stay temporarily, especially in a tent.
7. The holes in needles for passing thread through.
9. A device producing light.
11. To stop so somebody can catch up.
12. To pay out money.
14. Organ of vision and sight.
15. To move to and fro.
17. Towards the west when facing north.

Down

1. Front of the human head.
3. Contest of speed.
4. Moist, slightly wet.
6. A regular payment for the right to use something.
8. To put away for future use.
9. A polite dignified woman.
10. To not hit the target.
11. A bird's feathered limb used for flying.
13. To put something into the ground to grow.

Down (continued)

15. Used or used up.
16. Rear movable part of an animal's body.

29

Mystery Letter

Score /20

lamp	camp	
damp	rent	
spent	spend	
wing	swing	

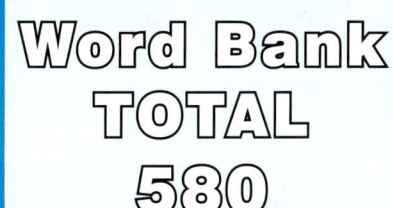

Exercise 29a

1) On holiday my dad decided to _____ a car for a few days.

2) The old _____ uses her trolley when she goes shopping.

3) He asked his mummy to push him on the _____ .

4) She put out the washing to dry but when she took it in it was still _____ .

5) Every summer I _____ for a week with my Scout troop.

6) The horse kept swishing his _____ to keep away the flies.

7) After my birthday I had to decide how to _____ the money I had been given.

8) I had a window seat looking out over the _____ of the aircraft.

9) The squirrel hides a large _____ of nuts before the winter.

10) He had his _____ closed but I knew he was not really asleep.

Score ___/10

Exercise 29b

11) At the junction the car turned _____ , away from the town centre.

12) She turned to _____ me and I saw she was laughing.

13) My sister and I gave mum a pot _____ for Mother's Day.

14) I went to the fair and _____ more on the rides than I had intended.

15) "_____ there and don't move," he called angrily.

16) It was a close _____ but I just managed to beat him.

17) The _____ fell off the table and the bulb was broken.

18) I could have taken _____ but there were too many for me to carry.

19) "I've got my _____ on you so make sure you behave yourself."

20) Since my friend moved away I really _____ her.

Score ___/10

sting	stamp	string
west	spin	skin
plan	rock	lock
clock	lump	pump

Exercise 30a

1) Dad sprayed his _____ tree to protect the fruit from pests and disease.

2) One of the popular places to visit in Australia is Ayers _____ .

3) He tried to _____ the ball with his bat but it went past and hit the wicket.

4) It was amazing to watch a spider _____ its web.

5) A large _____ of ice broke off the glacier and fell into the sea.

6) We were shown where to _____ our coats in the cloakroom.

7) The sun rises in the east and sets in the _____ .

8) She uses special mounts to _____ the stamps into her album.

9) The knife was _____ and would not cut the rope.

10) It was hard work to _____ and hoe the garden flower beds.

Score /10

Exercise 30b

11) She wrapped the parcel and tied _____ around it to make it more secure.

12) The _____ struck three but it was two minutes fast.

13) I felt the wasp _____ me and my finger began to swell up.

14) The groundsman sprinkled grass _____ on the bare patches.

15) They had a _____ but it was impossible to carry it out.

16) Before leaving home I had to _____ up the tyres on my bicycle.

17) Her nose _____ would not stop so they took her to hospital.

18) I put a _____ on the envelope and posted the letter yesterday.

19) The key for the _____ was missing and we could not get in.

20) Always use suncream to protect your _____ from the sun's rays.

Score /10

Word Bank

blunt, stick, seed, bleed, block, plum, weed, hang

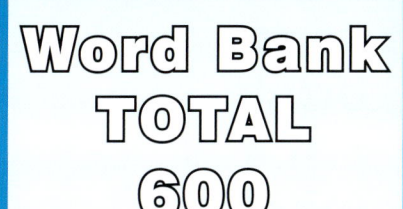

TOTAL 600

30

Across

1. Fruit of the grass plant.
2. Compass point opposite east.
4. To lose blood.
6. Round or oval edible fruit containing a flattened stone.
9. Drawing showing the layout of something.
10. To prevent movement through, into or out of something.
12. Turn round and round quickly.
13. Strong thin cord.
14. A large stone or boulder.
15. Natural layer covering an animal's body.
16. To suspend from above.

Down

1. Action of banging down a foot.
2. Wild plant growing where it is not wanted.
3. To force a liquid or gas to flow in a particular direction.
5. Mechanism to fasten a door and operated with a key.
7. A small solid chunk.
8. Not sharp.
11. A device displaying the time.
12. Thin branch or shoot from a tree.
15. To prick the skin and inject poison.

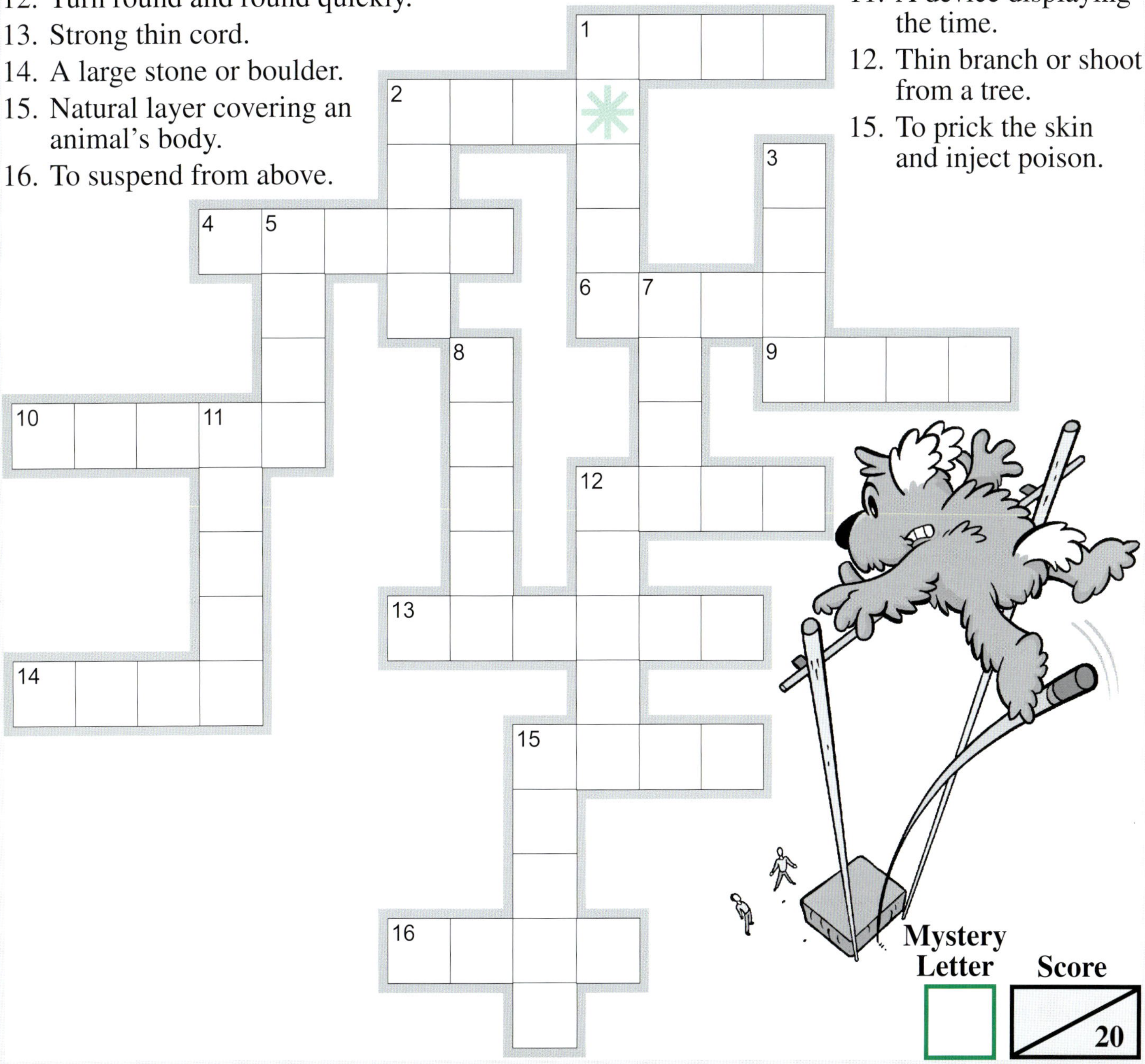

Mystery Letter

Score / 20

© 2005 Stephen Curran

sang	rang	pick
brick	trick	seem
pack	crack	pond
fond	chop	rush

Exercise 31a

1) He had overslept and had to _____ to catch his train.

2) The fox had been killing the farmer's chickens and it had to be _____ .

3) I helped my mother _____ the suitcases ready for our holiday.

4) She _____ in the church choir every Sunday.

5) Her husband and his team of campanologists _____ the church bells.

6) I am very _____ of pears but I prefer bananas.

7) The doorbell didn't _____ to be working so he used the knocker.

8) Last year we had none but this year the _____ is full of frogspawn.

9) The _____ in the wall extended from the floor to the ceiling.

10) She wrote a note to her aunt to _____ her for the present.

Score / 10

Exercise 31b

11) Robin Hood led a _____ of outlaws who lived in Sherwood Forest.

12) The boxer landed a punch to the _____ and his opponent was knocked out.

13) I hoped he would _____ me to play in the football team.

14) The shopkeeper went to the _____ to pay in yesterday's takings.

15) For my dinner I had a lamb _____ with potatoes, peas and gravy.

16) I watched the workmen build the new _____ wall and fit the gate.

17) _____ as he thought it had stopped, the rain started again.

18) She likes to _____ fresh oranges to extract the juice from them.

19) Producing a rabbit from a top hat is an old magic _____ .

20) "Look at the mess! Get the dustpan and _____ and clear it up."

Score / 10

Word Bank

brush, band, thank, shot, crush, bank, just, chin

Word Bank TOTAL 620

31

Across

3. Past tense of 'ring'.
4. Hard baked block used to build walls.
6. A very short time ago.
8. To move fast.
10. A firing of a gun.
12. Cut up something with downward strokes of a sharp tool.
14. A business that keeps money for people or companies.
15. To break without coming fully apart.
17. Put belongings into a bag for transporting.
18. Past tense of 'sing'.
19. Musicians playing together.

Down

1. A strong liking for something or somebody.
2. Tool with bristles used for painting and sweeping.
5. To squeeze and compress something.
7. Act of magic.
9. Appear to be something.
11. To express gratitude.
13. To choose.
16. Part of the face below the lips.
17. A pool of water often created artificially in a garden.

Don't forget to go back to page **3** and complete **Dickens's Mystery Word**.

Mystery Letter

Score /20

© 2005 Stephen Curran

17

At the Zoo

Can you find all these words in the picture below? Write the correct word against each number.

giraffe	tyre	broom	signpost	entrance
parrot	rhinoceros	kangaroo	camel	rope
gorilla	zoo keeper	polar bear	tiger	lions

1. _____ 2. _____ 3. _____
4. _____ 5. _____ 6. _____
7. _____ 8. _____ 9. _____
10. _____ 11. _____ 12. _____
13. _____ 14. _____ 15. _____

On the Farm

Can you find all these words in the picture below? Write in the correct word against each number. When you have finished you can colour in the picture if you want to.

tractor	pitchfork	piglet	farmer	churn
farmhouse	trough	fence	sheepdog	boot
chicken	barn	goat	crow	cart

1._____ 2._____ 3._____

4._____ 5._____ 6._____

7._____ 8._____ 9._____

10._____ 11._____ 12._____

13._____ 14._____ 15._____

© 2005 Stephen Curran

cave	wave	save
shell	smell	swell
dive	drive	driver
brave	crane	safe

Exercise 32a

1) They _____ together on the beach and watched the sun set on the horizon.

2) The van _____ unloaded the boxes and carried them into the building.

3) They used a very tall _____ to lift the heavy girders into place.

4) She enjoyed going to the computer _____ every Tuesday after school.

5) It is illegal to _____ foxes using hounds.

6) There were many yachts and motor boats on the _____ .

7) We use a breadmaker to _____ fresh bread at weekends.

8) The lovely _____ of freshly baked bread fills the house.

9) They walked along the shore and discovered a _____ in the rocks.

10) She turned to _____ goodbye but he had gone.

Score /10

Exercise 32b

11) He hid in the loft and thought he was _____ from capture.

12) He had been very _____ when rescuing the children and was given a medal.

13) She opened the mussel _____ but it was empty.

14) The _____ saw the injured animal, took aim and fired his rifle.

15) I always _____ my favourite black fruit gums till last.

16) His fishing _____ caught in the trees overhead when he cast his line.

17) Her ankle began to _____ when she sprained it while dancing.

18) They decided not to _____ but to go on the bus instead.

19) "Don't _____ into the pool until you know it's deep enough!"

20) She pulled the _____ over her head when it started to snow.

Score /10

© 2005 Stephen Curran

Word Bank

hood stood
hook club
hunt hunter
lake bake

TOTAL 640

32

Across

1. A person or animal that pursues birds or animals for food or sport.
2. Loose covering for the head.
3. Past tense of 'stand'.
6. Not in danger.
8. Large hollow in rock or underground.
9. Outer covering of an egg.
11. Control the movement of a vehicle.
12. Having or showing courage.
13. Large body of water surrounded by land.
14. Odour, stink, stench, aroma or perfume.

Down

1. Bent piece of metal used to fasten or lift another object.
2. To search for something that is difficult to find.
3. Become larger than normal.
4. Somebody who can operate a motor vehicle.
5. To cook food in an oven.
7. Thick stick used as a weapon.
8. Lifting machine.
9. Rescue somebody or something.
10. Move the hand repeatedly as a greeting, farewell or signal.
11. Jump head first into the water.

Put the mystery letters (*) from puzzles **32** to **38** into their numbered box below then rearrange them to make **Kate's Mystery Word**. The clue is **SCHOOL**.

Score: 20

Enter your mystery letters here:
32 33 34 35 36 37 38

Now rearrange them to make the:

Mystery Word:

© 2005 Stephen Curran

baker rise sake
spoon meet street
sheet rake wake
awake lift list

Across

1. A thin fog.
3. Eating utensil.
6. To come across, or get together.
8. Long-handled toothed gardening tool.
9. The good or welfare of somebody.
12. A series of related words, names or numbers arranged in order.
13. Day, month and year.
16. End somebody's or your own sleep.
17. A period of seven consecutive days.
18. Stand up or get higher.

Down

2. Cloth used on a bed.
4. A dish from which food is eaten.
5. What something or somebody is called.
7. The number between two and four.
9. A road in a town.
10. Dislike intensely.
11. Honey-making insect that can sting.
12. To raise to a higher position.
14. Somebody who makes bread and cakes.
15. Not asleep.

mist   week
three   named
date   hate
plate   bee

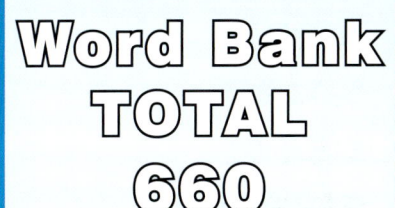

Exercise 33a

1) The queen _____ continually lays eggs in the hive.

2) The _____ Musketeers is a famous novel by Alexandre Dumas.

3) The waiter dropped the dinner _____ and it smashed on the floor.

4) The _____ worked all night making bread for the morning.

5) She checked the _____ in her diary and made a note of it.

6) She took the dirty _____ off the bed and put it in the wash.

7) Our neighbours held a _____ party to celebrate the Queen's Jubilee.

8) "Are you _____ ? It's time to get up."

9) She _____ the ship and broke a bottle of champagne on its bow.

10) I _____ being late for school but the bus didn't come today.

Score /10

Exercise 33b

11) The yeast in the dough makes the bread _____ .

12) Once a _____ his dad takes him swimming at the local baths.

13) "For goodness _____ Stephen, pay attention!"

14) The _____ was so thick the farmer could not see across his field.

15) Knife to the right, fork to the left and _____ across the top.

16) She made a _____ of all the films she had seen that year.

17) They took the _____ to the fourth floor of the hospital.

18) He went to bed late and didn't _____ up until ten next morning.

19) "We'll _____ you on the corner by the pillar box at three o'clock."

20) The gardener used a _____ to gather up the leaves.

Score /10

© 2005 Stephen Curran

free	queen	fine
shine	pine	mate
case	chase	creep
sleep	asleep	chain

Exercise 34a

1) The king or _____ of Great Britain is crowned in Westminster Abbey.

2) He was _____ a very pretty picture with many bright colours.

3) A policewoman ran after the thief and passers-by joined in the _____ .

4) "We can talk more about this _____ we are walking to school."

5) He used a padlock and _____ to secure his bike to the railings.

6) My dog's legs twitch while he's _____ . My dad says he's dreaming.

7) We collected old newspapers and the _____ grew bigger and bigger.

8) Our class studied the cones from _____ trees.

9) While I was running I had a _____ in my side. My teacher called it a stitch.

10) The wax polish made his car _____ like new.

Score / 10

Exercise 34b

11) Entry to the castle was _____ for children under five years old.

12) It was a _____ and sunny day with a light breeze.

13) The first _____ ordered the ship's crew to hoist the sails.

14) When his _____ came to trial he was found guilty and sentenced.

15) They used a pale blue _____ to decorate the bathroom walls.

16) "_____ in quietly and check if the baby is still awake."

17) "I have checked and she's _____ peacefully in her cot."

18) They had new bunk beds and his brother wanted to _____ in the top one.

19) We were _____ on the platform for the train to London.

20) She gave him a lovely _____ and he smiled back at her.

Score / 10

24 © 2005 Stephen Curran

pain   paint
pile   smile
while   sleeping
painting   waiting

Across

34

2. Doing nothing expecting something to happen.
3. Cash paid as a punishment if somebody breaks the law.
6. State of not being awake during which the body rests.
8. To connect or join two things together.
10. A pleasant facial expression.
11. Move quietly.
13. Not awake.
16. At or during the same time.
17. A picture made using paint.
18. Woman ruler.

Down

1. Feeling of discomfort in a particular part of the body.
3. Costing nothing.
4. A piece of luggage or something that serves as a container.
5. A series of joined metal rings.
7. A mound of things heaped or stacked on top of each other.
9. To yearn or long for somebody.
11. Try to catch or overtake somebody.

Down (continued)

12. To be in a state of sleep or dormant.
14. Coloured liquid applied to a surface to decorate or protect it.
15. To give out light.

Mystery Letter

Score /20

© 2005 Stephen Curran

cost	frost	frog
wide	slide	life
lace	place	grand
wife	son	grandfather

35

Across

4. Amount paid for something.
6. A female, alone and unaided.
9. With sides or edges far apart.
11. A long slim connecting part of an object.
12. To press against something in order to move it.
13. An outdoor temperature below freezing point.
14. Outstanding and impressive in appearance.
15. Wished that something would be true.
16. Delicate fabric with patterned holes.
17. The woman to whom a particular man is married.
19. A male child in relation to his parents.

Down

1. A male, alone and unaided.
2. Night-flying insect resembling a butterfly.
3. The whole time somebody is alive.
5. The father of your mother or father.

Down (continued)

7. Refers back to the speaker or writer.
8. A woody branched plant that is smaller than a tree.
10. To move smoothly across a surface.
12. Area or portion of space.
18. Small web-footed water animal.

Mystery Letter

Score 20

26 © 2005 Stephen Curran

push   bush
stem   myself
herself   himself
moth   hoped

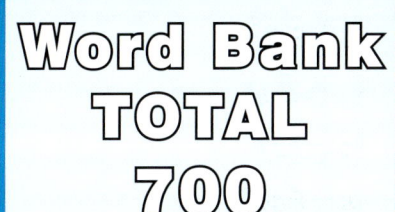

Exercise 35a

1) My _____ told me there were no mobile phones when he was a boy.

2) She managed to struggle home with it all by _____ .

3) I couldn't believe a new bike would _____ so much money.

4) My little sister prefers the _____ to the swings in the children's playground.

5) She always asks me to _____ her when she is on the swing.

6) The _____ was attracted to the bright light from the lantern.

7) He married his _____ over thirty five years ago.

8) They had a _____ and three daughters.

9) It was too _____ to jump across so we had to walk round it.

10) She had _____ to buy a new one but they had sold out.

Score ___/10

Exercise 35b

11) I was left by _____ and my parents didn't come back for several hours.

12) The _____ was too tall and thick and had to be pruned.

13) He heard a noise but there was no one but _____ in the room.

14) The _____ of the wine glass was very tall and slender.

15) It was a very cold night and _____ covered the ground.

16) The old house was very _____ and it's owners must have been very wealthy.

17) During her long _____ she had done many wonderful things.

18) He returned to the _____ where he had lost his wallet but could not find it.

19) The _____'s two large eyes could be seen just above the water.

20) The tablecloth was made of _____ and was very pretty.

Score ___/10

© 2005 Stephen Curran

kiss	itself	neck
body	fold	scold
held	mind	wild
child	snap	strap

Exercise 36a

1) By _____ it wasn't worth much but it completed the set.

2) I had to buy a new _____ for my watch because the old one broke.

3) The school _____ were very excited but well behaved.

4) The driver sounded his _____ to warn the pedestrians.

5) He was _____ with a white stick and he asked me to help him cross the road.

6) I _____ his arm and led him across when the road was clear.

7) Although her coat was very _____ she was shivering with the cold.

8) He went to _____ the ball but it bounced and went past him.

9) It was a _____ night with howling wind, rough sea and driving rain.

10) She put a silk scarf around her _____ before she put her coat on.

Score /10

Exercise 36b

11) She picked him up, gave him a _____ and he shrieked with delight.

12) There was _____ car just like his parked nearby.

13) We drove past the _____ of a dead badger on the roadside.

14) The young _____ was lost and crying for its mother.

15) Although she quite liked _____ skirts, she decided not to buy either of them.

16) She asked him to _____ the tablecloth and put it in the drawer.

17) His teacher had to _____ him when he misbehaved in class.

18) Her cat began to _____ her hand and its tongue felt very rough.

19) I don't _____ helping my dad in the garden. In fact I enjoy it.

20) They heard the twig _____ under his foot and knew where he was.

Score /10

© 2005 Stephen Curran

Word Bank

both, children, lick, thick, blind, another, kick, horn

TOTAL 720

36

Across

4. Break with a sharp noise.
7. Noise-making warning device.
9. Touch with the lips.
11. Young human being.
12. To tell somebody off.
13. Deep or broad.
15. Past tense of 'hold'.
17. Two things considered together.
18. To watch over and look after.
19. Bend something thin and flat over on itself.

Down

1. Unable to see.
2. Sons or daughters of human parents.
3. One more.
5. Joins the head to the rest of the body.
6. Strike with the foot.
8. Not tame or domesticated.
10. Loop of flexible material used as a handle.
14. Used to refer back to something or for emphasis.
16. Pass the tongue over something.
17. The main part of the human body, not including the head, arms or legs.

Mystery Letter

Score /20

© 2005 Stephen Curran

born	gas	crab
swim	storm	quick
joy	ticket	park
bark	mark	tea

Across

37

2. Upright pole of wood or metal fixed in the ground.
4. A crustacean with a broad flat shell, antennae and claws.
6. A spot, a scratch or dirty patch.
7. Moving or doing something fast.
10. To move yourself through water using natural means.
11. Gathering for buying and selling.
13. A substance that is neither a solid nor a liquid.
14. Plant's dried leaves used to make a drink by adding boiling water.
15. To give lessons in a subject.
17. The angle formed where two or more lines or surfaces meet.

Down

1. Violent weather with strong winds, rain, sleet, snow or hail.
2. To stop and leave a motor vehicle beside or off the road.
3. Noise made by dog or fox.
5. Brought into life.
8. Any cereal crop, especially wheat, barley or oats.
9. Travel pass.
10. Base of a tree trunk and its roots after it has been felled.
11. Nearly all or the majority.
12. Somebody who shows somebody how to do something.
16. Great happiness or pleasure.

Mystery Letter

Score 20

teach	teacher
most	post
stump	market
corn	corner

Exercise 37a

1) The box had been dropped and one _____ was damaged.

2) He was _____ in Leeds but his family moved to Lincoln soon after.

3) His _____ showed the date, flight and seat number.

4) "Can you _____?" asked the attendant. "If not, stay in the shallow end."

5) My parents saw my maths _____ who said she was very pleased with me.

6) Tuesday is _____ day in the village and it's really busy.

7) She went shopping in the car but there was nowhere to _____ .

8) One of my favourite starters is _____ on the cob covered with butter.

9) We soon cut down the tree but the _____ took ages to dig up.

10) She went to _____ the letter but missed the last collection.

Score /10

Exercise 37b

11) The _____ of the tree was covered in moss and its trunk looked green.

12) "Don't light a match, I think I can smell _____ !"

13) The fishmonger dressed the _____ and removed the meat from its shell.

14) It was a violent _____ and the lifeboat was launched twice that night.

15) I had a professional coach to _____ me to play tennis.

16) It was so _____ it was over before I knew it!

17) I don't know about your friends, but _____ of mine have got a mobile phone.

18) She scored the top _____ in the test with eighteen out of twenty.

19) It was a _____ to see him looking so well after his long illness.

20) "Make me a nice cup of _____ please, I'm gasping."

Score /10

© 2005 Stephen Curran

poor	**door**	**floor**
roof	**doze**	**dozing**
poking	**joking**	**storing**
boring	**loving**	**prune**

Exercise 38a

1) She was so _____ she couldn't afford to heat her home properly.

2) The film was so _____ I left the cinema before it ended.

3) Jack kept _____ me in the back with a ruler all through the lesson.

4) At Christmas our class gave the kitchen _____ a tin of sweets to thank them.

5) He climbed onto the _____ to put up the new television aerial.

6) She was very fond of her pony and gave him a _____ pat on his neck.

7) The trees in our street needed _____ as they had grown so high.

8) Penicillin, used for _____ infections, was discovered by Alexander Fleming.

9) The cat was lying in the garden and _____ in the sun.

10) "Please close the classroom _____ behind you, William."

Score ⬜ 10

Exercise 38b

11) Pipes that were once made of metal are now made from plastic _____ .

12) They pulled the _____ and in it was a paper hat, a small gift and a silly joke.

13) The piano in our school hall badly needed _____ and it sounded quite strange.

14) It was a still evening and the hot-air _____ floated by silently overhead.

15) My dad always has a short _____ in the armchair after Sunday lunch.

16) He went to the fair and bought a _____ apple on a stick.

17) My teacher said I was very rude but I told him I was only _____ .

18) He used a special saw and secateurs to _____ the trees.

19) He played with his train set on the _____ .

20) He used the boxes for _____ old magazines in his loft.

Score ⬜ 10

Word Bank

pruning, tuning, toffee, balloon, tubing, curing, staff, cracker

TOTAL 760

38

Across

2. A coloured rubber or plastic bag inflated with air or helium.
3. A large heavy stick used for support when walking.
7. Healing.
10. A plum preserved by drying.
12. Movable panel used to open and close the entrance of a building.
13. Have a short light sleep.
15. The flat horizontal part of a room to walk on.
16. Holding something somewhere for safekeeping.
18. Uninteresting.
19. Saying or doing things to make people laugh.

Down

1. A soft and chewy or hard and brittle sweet.
4. Hollow, cylindrical material that tubes are made of.
5. Prodding with something.
6. Flat crisp biscuit often eaten with cheese.
8. Outside covering of the top of a building.
9. Showing or feeling affection.
10. Cutting branches away to encourage growth.
11. Spending time lazily or in a daydream.
14. Opposite of rich.
17. Adjusting the pitch of a musical instrument.

Don't forget to go back to page **21** and complete **Kate's Mystery Word**.

Mystery Letter

Score /20

© 2005 Stephen Curran

At the Airport

Can you find all these words in the picture below? Write the correct word against each number.

trolley	litter bin	rucksack	check-in	aeroplane
briefcase	aircrew	duty-free	radar	loudspeaker
girders	passport	wing	label	ticket

1. _____ 2. _____ 3. _____
4. _____ 5. _____ 6. _____
7. _____ 8. _____ 9. _____
10. _____ 11. _____ 12. _____
13. _____ 14. _____ 15. _____

At the Port

Can you find all these words in the picture below? Write in the correct word against each number. When you have finished you can colour in the picture if you want to.

hovercraft	cable	seagull	anchor	ramp
flag	warship	crane	jetty	buoy
crate	funnel	mast	sailor	portholes

1. _____ 2. _____ 3. _____

4. _____ 5. _____ 6. _____

7. _____ 8. _____ 9. _____

10. _____ 11. _____ 12. _____

13. _____ 14. _____ 15. _____

© 2005 Stephen Curran

sideboard	law	jaw
hawk	mummy	dummy
slammed	tummy	pinned
grinned	winner	winning

Exercise 39a

1) The fruit bowl was on the _____ and the cutlery was kept in the drawer.

2) For many years she had recorded every day's events in her _____ .

3) The driver lost control and his car _____ into the back of the car in front.

4) His bicycle _____ was punctured and he had to buy a new inner tube.

5) She had lost weight and was much _____ than when he last saw her.

6) He could see a _____ hovering above its prey waiting to dive on it.

7) The solicitor had worked in the _____ firm for several years.

8) The stable lad took the racehorse from its _____ and put on the saddle.

9) It was very hot and the man selling ice _____ had a very good day.

10) He had eaten too much and his _____ felt very full.

Score / 10

Exercise 39b

11) The Egyptian _____ was found in the burial chamber of the pyramid.

12) His rear wheel had no _____ and his back was covered in mud.

13) My granddad used to tell me there were _____ at the bottom of his garden.

14) She _____ the notice on the wall for everyone to see.

15) They were very happy with the result and _____ at each other.

16) By _____ the match they qualified for the final.

17) She opened her new _____ and wrote the first entry for that year.

18) The baby's _____ had been dropped on the floor and needed to be washed.

19) In the accident his _____ was broken when his face hit the ground.

20) The lottery _____ received nearly three million pounds.

Score / 10

Word Bank

thinner, fairies, diaries, tyre, diary, lollies, stall, mudguard

TOTAL 780

39

Across

1. A binding and enforceable rule of conduct.
4. Tooth bearing bones.
5. Piece of dining room furniture with flat top, drawers and cupboards.
8. A compartment for a single large animal.
10. Ahead of the others during a race.
11. Mother.
12. Several books containing personal records of events in somebody's life.
13. Smiled broadly.
14. Bird of prey with talons that hunts in the daytime.
15. Somebody's stomach.
16. A model of a human used for displaying clothes.
17. Fastened with pins.

Down

1. Lollipops.
2. Someone who beats every opponent in a competition or fight.
3. Imaginary beings with magic powers.
6. Less thick.
7. Closed forcefully and noisily.
9. A curved rigid arch above the wheel of a bicycle or motorcycle.
12. Book for keeping notes of appointments or recording events.
15. Hollow band of rubber fitted around the edge of a wheel and filled with air.

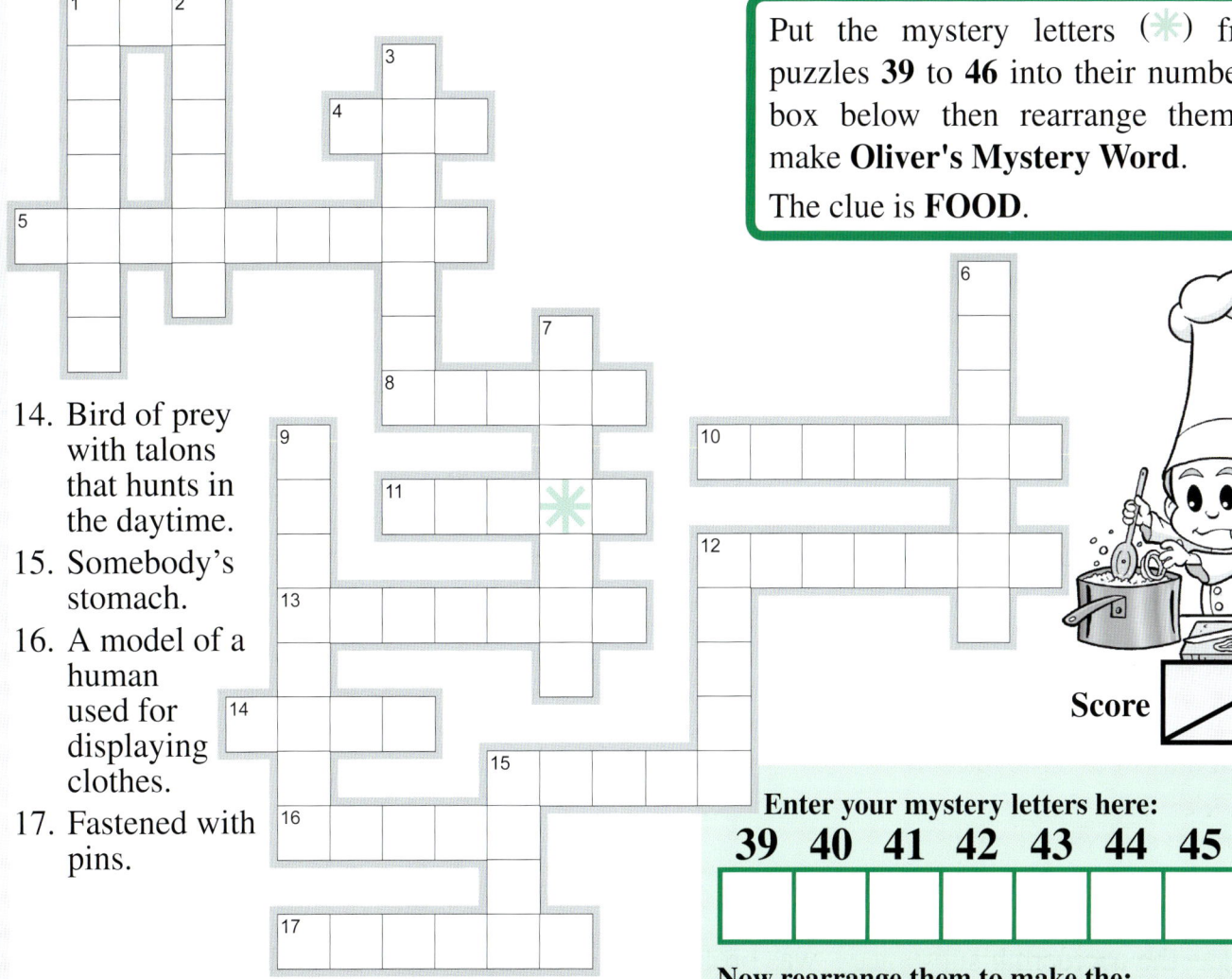

Put the mystery letters (✱) from puzzles **39** to **46** into their numbered box below then rearrange them to make **Oliver's Mystery Word**.

The clue is **FOOD**.

Score / 20

Enter your mystery letters here:
39 40 41 42 43 44 45 46

Now rearrange them to make the:

Mystery Word:

© 2005 Stephen Curran

handpump   handlebars   spanner
pedal   oilcan   wax
foxes   fried   lied
freckle   prickle   trace

Across   40

1. Device for inflating bicycle tyres.
6. A sharp pointed projection on the outer surface of a leaf or plant.
9. Small orange-red fish kept in aquariums and ponds.
12. A metal container with a long thin spout holding lubricating oil.

Down

2. A small round stone.
3. Distance covered in a single step or stride.
4. Cooked quickly in fat.
5. Causing discomfort or pain by repeatedly scraping the skin.
7. Move in a swaying, trembling, shaking way.
8. A thin film of something filled with air.
10. A tool used to grasp, turn or twist objects such as nuts and bolts.
11. Wild animals of the dog family with long bushy tail.
13. A person who makes or mends shoes.
15. To find out where somebody is.
18. Small yellow finch kept as a pet.

Across (continued)

14. A foot-operated lever.
16. Used to steer a bicycle or motorcycle.
17. Brown spot on the skin.
19. Deliberately said something that was not true.
20. Naturally-occurring substance that feels greasy or oily to the touch.

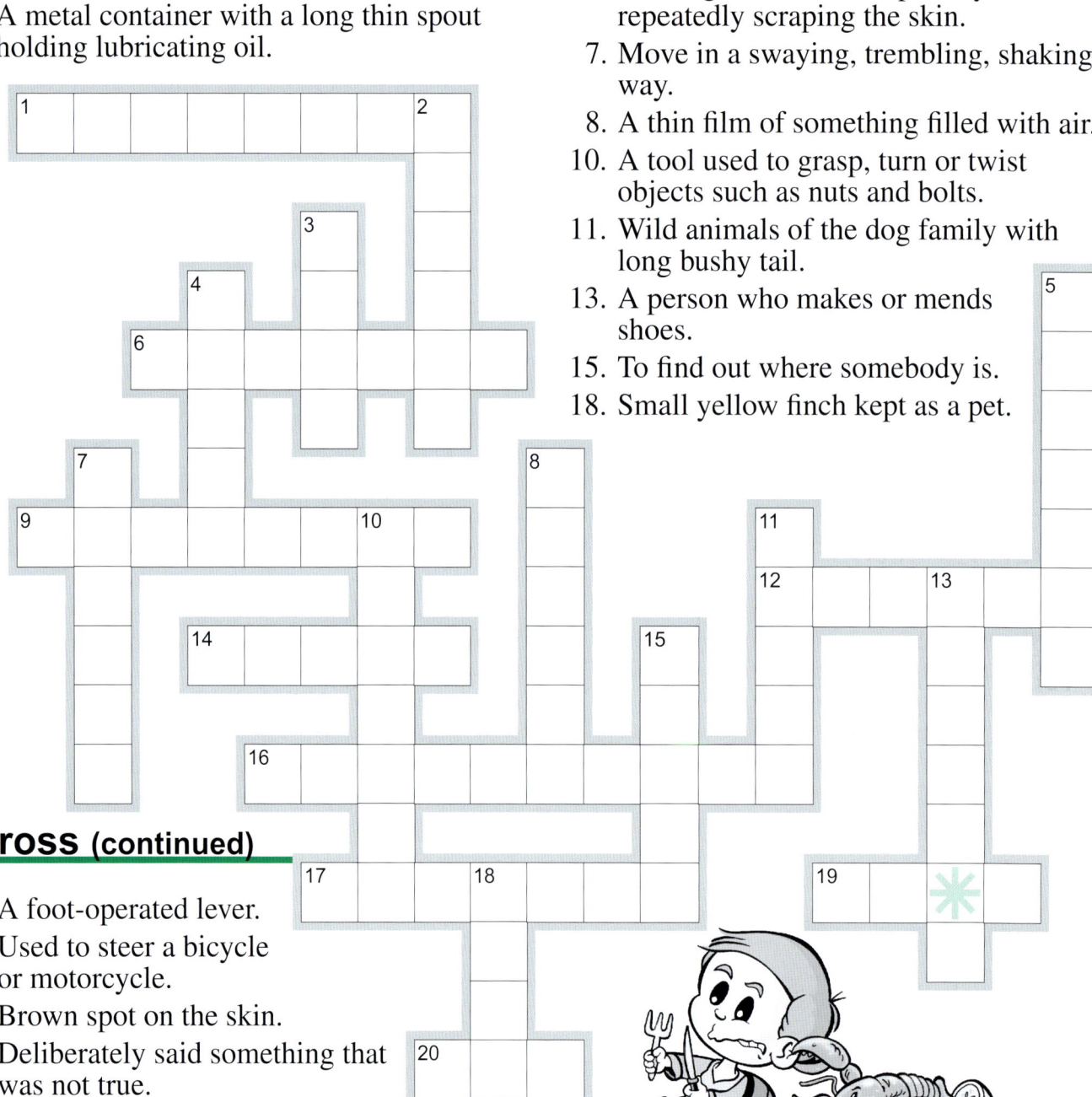

Mystery Letter

Score /20

© 2005 Stephen Curran

pace　　　　　cobbler
rubbing　　　bubble
pebble　　　　wobble
canary　　　　goldfish

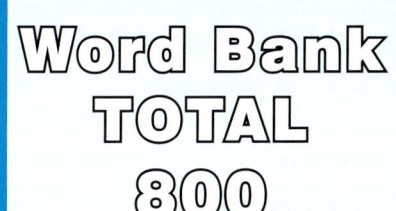

Word Bank TOTAL 800

Exercise 40a

1) The cat sat and watched the _____ swimming round the bowl.

2) He _____ and said he had not seen it when clearly he had.

3) He asked the _____ to put new soles and heels on his black shoes.

4) He refilled his _____ and continued to lubricate all the moving parts.

5) The ground was uneven and her bicycle began to _____ dangerously.

6) My _____ was missing and I had to use John's to inflate my tyre.

7) He tried to make the flat _____ skim across the surface of the lake.

8) We kept very still and watched the _____ crossing the field ahead.

9) I prefer _____ eggs to boiled ones.

10) His hearing was poor due to a build up of _____ in his ears.

Score /10

Exercise 40b

11) She was very tired and kept _____ her eyes with her hands.

12) The cyclist hit the car so hard that he was thrown over his _____ .

13) My grandma's _____ is bright yellow and sings very noisily.

14) He had not got a _____ to fit the nut and could not undo it.

15) The runners were setting a fast _____ and a new record looked possible.

16) The rash looked very red and his hand began to _____ .

17) He asked the genealogist to _____ his ancestors and prepare a family tree.

18) The water neared boiling point and began to _____ .

19) She had a large _____ right in the centre of her forehead.

20) He began to _____ quickly after the other cyclists.

Score /10

© 2005 Stephen Curran

budgerigar	toddler	assistant
handbag	whale	eyebrows
seaweed	shovel	strict
kerb	pillar box	policeman

Exercise 41a

1) *Moby Dick* is a novel about Captain Ahab and the great white _____ .

2) Everything had been sold and the _____ were empty.

3) The _____ used his radio to call for an ambulance.

4) I looked after my neighbour's _____ and he flew out of his cage.

5) He had dark, bushy _____ and looked quite menacing.

6) The _____ flew very low across the airfield and the pilot waved.

7) The road _____ sharply to the left and the approaching car could not be seen.

8) "Take this _____ and help to clear the snow from the path."

9) The stall was _____ doughnuts and the smell filled the air.

10) The newborn _____ were in the cowshed with their mothers.

Score / 10

Exercise 41b

11) _____ hunt together in packs.

12) A mother with a _____ was waiting at the crossing.

13) She lifted him up so he could put the letter into the _____ .

14) He saved up to buy an electric _____ and amplifier.

15) It was a high _____ at the side of the road and her wheelchair could not get up it.

16) "Can I help you?" asked the shop _____ .

17) The rough sea had swept a lot of _____ onto the beach.

18) They arranged a _____ party for her eightieth birthday.

19) The rules were very _____ and we had to agree to obey them.

20) Her _____ was black and made from real leather.

Score / 10

© 2005 Stephen Curran

guitar aircraft
curved surprise
frying wolves
calves shelves

Word Bank TOTAL 820

Across **41**

2. Long-handled scoop for lifting and moving loose material.
5. Severe in maintaining discipline or ensuring that rules are obeyed.
7. Small bright green parrot with a yellow head kept as a pet.
10. Cooking in fat over a high heat.
11. Plants such as kelp that grow in the sea.
14. Carnivores related to the dog and hunt in packs.
16. Large marine mammal that breathes through a blowhole.
17. Young child who is learning to walk.
18. Helper.

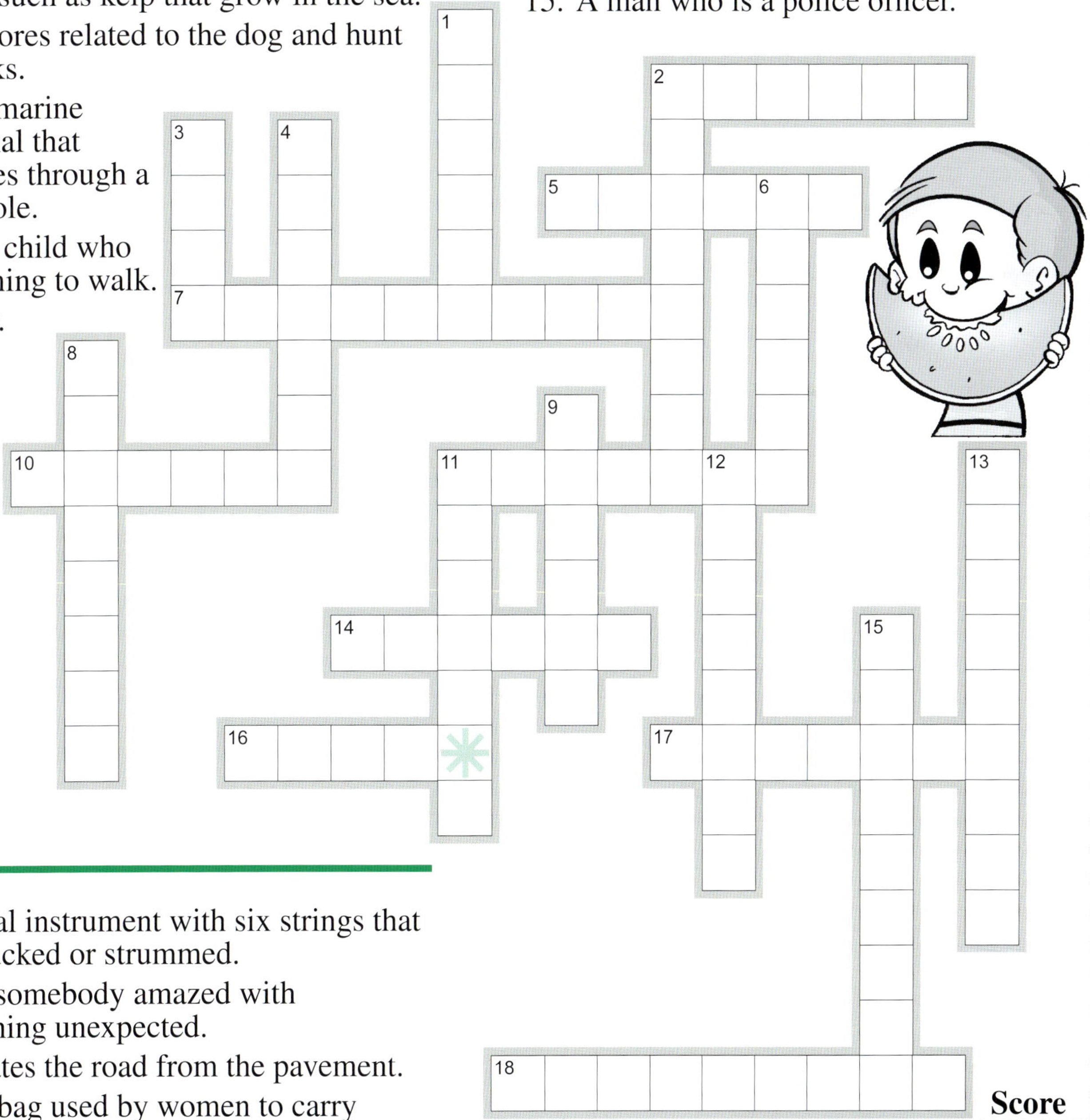

Down (continued)

8. Any vehicle capable of flight.
9. Young cows or bulls.
11. Flat rectangular boards, usually attached to a wall, used for storing or displaying objects.
12. Hair above the eye socket.
13. Collection point for letters to be posted.
15. A man who is a police officer.

Down

1. Musical instrument with six strings that are plucked or strummed.
2. Make somebody amazed with something unexpected.
3. Separates the road from the pavement.
4. Small bag used by women to carry personal items.
6. Rounded.

Mystery Letter **Score /20**

© 2005 Stephen Curran 41

itches scratches hutch
greenhouse wheelbarrow sundial
bonfire trowel sunflowers
rockery purrs worried

Across

5. Heavy, double-hooked device for holding a ship in place.
6. An irritating sensation that causes a desire to scratch the skin.
8. Small hand tool used by gardeners for light digging.
9. Area of a garden that has large stones in it with low-growing plants.
11. Small animal shelter made from wood and wire.
12. Somebody who prepares a text for publication.
13. Fiery mass of rock from space.
15. Tall plants with a large yellow flower and edible seeds that yield oil.
17. Dishonest person who steals.
19. Rotating part of a machine.
20. Small-flowered evergreen shrub that grows on heaths and mountainsides.

Down

1. An instrument that shows the time by using a sun-generated shadow.
2. Slight cut or marks on a surface.
3. Outside fire used to burn rubbish.
4. Strike heavily with fist or an object.
7. Glass hothouse used for growing plants.
10. Small cart with only one wheel.
14. Rushes to do something.
16. To feel anxious about something.
18. To emit the low murmuring noise that cats make.

Mystery Letter

Score 20

hurries	thump
meteor	anchor
rotor	editor
heather	crook

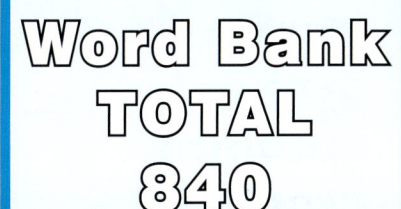

Word Bank TOTAL 840

Exercise 42a

1) "Don't scratch!" she shouted. "But it really _____ ," he moaned.

2) The _____ blades turned and lifted the helicopter from the ship's deck.

3) We planted _____ and they grew over two metres tall.

4) There was a loud _____ and a cloud of dust when the sack hit the floor.

5) The heath was covered with _____ coloured purple and pink.

6) Pieces of the _____ fell to earth after it had broken up in the atmosphere.

7) The ship dropped _____ and remained offshore for the night.

8) The seedlings grown in the _____ were planted out in the garden.

9) The workman pushed the _____ up the ramp to fill the skip.

10) _____ Night is the 5th of November.

Score /10

Exercise 42b

11) The thorns were very sharp and he had deep _____ on both his arms.

12) My brother is a newspaper _____ and decides which stories are reported.

13) The shepherd used his _____ to lift the lamb to safety.

14) When I stroke my cat it _____ very loudly.

15) "Don't look so _____ , it might never happen!"

16) He cleaned out the rabbit's _____ and put in fresh straw, food and water.

17) The farmer _____ to finish the harvesting before the weather changes.

18) He built a _____ and planted small flowers between the large stones.

19) The shadow from the _____'s gnomon showed three o'clock.

20) She dug holes with a _____ to plant the tulip bulbs.

Score /10

© 2005 Stephen Curran

brook	rook	bride
brake	crisps	crayons
crocodile	creak	crawl
crop	cast	tick

Exercise 43a

1) She drew a very colourful picture with her new _____ .

2) He wore a white _____ with the company's name printed on the back.

3) During our trip to Holland we visited a traditional _____ maker.

4) Sarah carefully spread the glue and sprinkled _____ onto the card.

5) After the heavy rainfall the little _____ was full of water.

6) After the wet winter and warm summer the _____ was better than usual.

7) The _____ and her father were driven to her wedding in an open-topped car.

8) "_____ your net to the right side," Jesus told Simon Peter.

9) The potholer had to _____ on all fours along the low passage.

10) The warm _____ from the fire made the room feel really cosy.

Score /10

Exercise 43b

11) The hinges were dry and the door gave a loud _____ as she opened it.

12) High in the tree the nests of a _____ colony could be seen.

13) The _____ seized its prey in its powerful jaws and rolled in the water.

14) She had to _____ suddenly and her seatbelt saved her life.

15) My favourite flavour of _____ is cheese and onion.

16) A short _____ from the film was shown in the programme.

17) By scaling the steep _____ with ropes the commandos surprised the enemy.

18) Once she could swim the _____ of the pool she tried to complete a length.

19) "If your answer is correct put a _____ against it."

20) There was a loud _____ but the gun failed to fire.

Score /10

tee shirt	width
clip	cliff
clog	click
glow	glitter

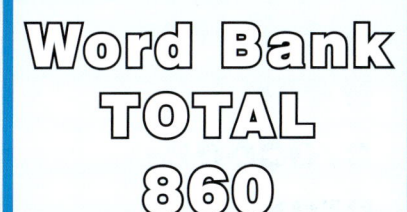

Across 43

3. Small stream.
5. A soft, steady light.
6. High steep rock face extending along a coastline.
7. A recurring clicking sound as made by a clock.
9. To throw a baited fishing line into the water.
11. Large tropical reptile with strong jaws that lives near water.
14. Bird of the crow family.
16. Collarless short-sleeved cotton shirt.
17. Device to slow or stop a machine.

Down

1. To block a tube or opening gradually with dirt or dust.
2. Move along slowly close to the ground.
4. Sticks of coloured wax used for drawing and colouring.
5. To sparkle or shimmer brightly.
6. Plants grown for use.
8. A short sharp sound.
9. To cut or trim something.
10. A woman at her wedding.
12. Very thin fried potato slice eaten as a snack.
13. A prolonged squeaking noise.
15. The distance from one side to the other.

© 2005 Stephen Curran

gladiator **gloss** **glare**
frock **freezer** **frighten**
fringe **fridge** **groom**
gravy **grin** **grab**

44

Across

2. A loose baggy outer garment with sleeves.
5. Sports shoes with a thick sole.
7. Smile broadly showing the teeth.
8. To shine brightly and intensely.
9. The shine on a smooth surface.
13. A fighter in a Roman arena.
15. Sauce made with meat juices.
17. Someone diving underwater with flippers, a mask and a snorkel.
18. Refrigerated cabinet where frozen food is stored.

Down

1. Someone using roller skates or ice skates.
3. Glide over the snow on skis.

Down (continued)

4. Hair cut to fall over the forehead.
6. A route through the countryside.
7. To make a noise like a pig.
8. To clean and brush or comb an animal.
10. Very thin.
11. An uncontrolled slide.
12. To make somebody afraid.
14. Grasp something quickly, suddenly, or forcefully.
16. A refrigerator.

Mystery Letter

Score /20

© 2005 Stephen Curran

grunt
trail
ski
skin diver
trainers
skater
skid
skinny

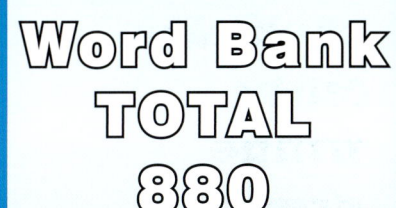

Exercise 44a

1) The dog was so _____ that its ribs could be seen quite clearly.

2) The _____ 's mask had fogged up so he had to surface.

3) We took three cartons of ice cream from the _____ .

4) He looked in the _____ but all the yoghurt had been eaten.

5) The beginners were taught to _____ on the nursery slopes.

6) The Romans enjoyed watching a _____ fighting a lion in the arena.

7) He gave a wide _____ and we could see he had several teeth missing.

8) "Don't throw stones into the river; you'll _____ the ducks."

9) Men wore a knee-length _____ coat in the 19th century.

10) Its _____ had grown so long you could hardly see its eyes.

Score /10

Exercise 44b

11) The ice _____ was very graceful and moved at great speed.

12) He followed the _____ left by the animal and discovered its lair.

13) The _____ mark showed where the coach had swerved and tried to stop.

14) His new _____ were much more comfortable to run in.

15) She tried to _____ the rail but missed and fell down the step.

16) For a while the _____ from the headlights blinded him.

17) "Would you please move the _____ boat to the other end of the table."

18) The new brand of paint had a tough finish with a very high _____ .

19) It is customary for the bride and _____ to have the first dance.

20) The pig gave a loud _____ and rolled back on its side.

Score /10

© 2005 Stephen Curran

skylark	cowboy	foil
curly	curry	whinny
whirl	whisk	slack
slam	slap	slate

Exercise 45a

1) High in the air he could see a _____ and hear its song.

2) He _____ the team to success last season but this year they failed to win.

3) The soft _____ of a horse could be heard in the still evening air.

4) She put the ticket into the _____ and the car park barrier lifted.

5) Many years ago children used chalk and a _____ in the classroom.

6) He took his _____ at the head of the table.

7) In Roman ships one _____ was often pulled by two or three galley slaves.

8) The steps of the harbour wall were covered in _____ and very slippery.

9) The chef used a fork to _____ the egg whites for the meringue.

10) My aunt knitted a new cosy for our _____ .

Score /10

Exercise 45b

11) The rope was too _____ so they pulled it tighter and secured it.

12) The snow was melting and _____ covered the pavement.

13) A line of type used to be set and cast as a _____ of hot-metal.

14) He congratulated his partner and gave him a _____ on the back.

15) She hated her _____ hair and tried all sorts of ways to straighten it.

16) A _____ looks after cattle and works on horseback or in a motor vehicle.

17) We used to collect silver _____ to raise money for charity.

18) _____ powder usually contains cumin, turmeric, coriander, chilli and ginger.

19) "Don't _____ the door; you'll wake the baby!"

20) My head was in a _____ and I felt quite dizzy.

Score /10

Word Bank

slime
slug
seat
oar
slot
slush
teapot
coached

TOTAL 900

Across 45

2. Like a snail but has no shell.
4. Cooking utensil for whipping something.
6. Melting snow or ice.
9. Container used for making and serving tea.
10. Man who looks after cattle.
12. Blow made with the open hand.
13. Curled or coiled.
14. Bird noted for its melodious singing while hanging high in the air.
15. To turn or spin rapidly.
16. A place to sit.

Down

1. Not tight or taut.
3. Narrow opening.
4. To neigh softly.
5. Slippery liquid unpleasant to touch.
7. A long thin sword used in fencing.

Down (continued)

8. Being trained in a sport, singing or acting.
10. Meat, fish or vegetables in a highly spiced sauce.
11. Used singly or in pairs in a rowing boat.
12. Roofing tile.
14. Close something noisily.

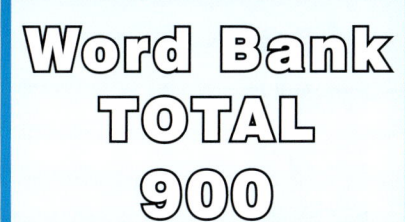

Mystery Letter

Score /20

stoat	poise	fake
male	kite	core
tone	cone	rule
mule	mute	lure

Exercise 46a

1) She rattled his dish to _____ her dog into the house.

2) The _____ has a brown coat and feeds on rabbits and other small mammals.

3) One _____ paddled hard across the pond to catch up with the rest.

4) A ballerina performs with grace and _____ when she dances.

5) Popular from the 14th to the 17th century, a _____ is a guitar-like instrument.

6) They searched the entire area but could find no sign of them _____ .

7) The violin was very old and had a wonderful sound and a rich _____ .

8) He pressed the _____ button on the TV remote control to switch off the sound.

9) He was taking his car to France so he put a 'GB' _____ on the back.

10) It was a secret and he couldn't tell _____ .

Score /10

Exercise 46b

11) It was a very hot day and she dropped another ice _____ into her drink.

12) The painting was thought to be by Constable but it was a _____ and worthless.

13) The Earth's _____ is molten in parts and composed of an alloy of iron and nickel.

14) "Don't touch that it's _____ and you'll get it all over your clothes!"

15) The sand _____ was made that high by the action of the wind.

16) He didn't buy a newspaper, as a _____ , but this was an exception.

17) The sign read: "OVERHEAD CABLES. _____ FLYING PROHIBITED".

18) A _____ duck is called a drake.

19) He rode one _____ and led another carrying his possessions.

20) Peter took a pine _____ to school for the nature table.

Score /10

50 © 2005 Stephen Curran

lute	dune
cube	anyone
anywhere	mucky
duckling	sticker

Word Bank TOTAL 920

Across

46

1. Cross between a female horse and a male donkey.
4. Any or every particular person.
7. Small mammal like a weasel.
8. A particular kind of sound.
9. A young duck.
11. Not genuine.
13. Relating to men or boys.
14. Filthy or very dirty.
15. Solid figure of six equal sides.
16. Hill of sand formed by wind or water action.
17. To govern.
18. The central or most important part of something.

Down

2. Attached to a fishing line to attract fish.
3. To place or hold something in balance or suspension.

Down (continued)

5. A toy for flying in the wind.
6. An adhesive label.
10. Musical instrument, like a guitar, which is plucked.
12. One or many places unknown.
13. Making no sound.
15. A pointed object with a round base.

! Don't forget to go back to page **37** and complete **Oliver's Mystery Word**.

Mystery Letter

Score / 20

© 2005 Stephen Curran

Book Two Word List

able	brush	creep	find
add	bubble	crisps	fine
after	budgerigar	crocodile	fire
again	bush	crook	first
aircraft	butter	crop	floor
anchor	calves	crush	fly
another	camp	cube	foil
anyone	canary	curing	fold
anywhere	case	curly	fond
apple	cast	curry	found
arm	cave	curved	foxes
ask	chain	damp	freckle
asleep	chair	dark	free
assistant	chase	date	freezer
ate	child	dear	fridge
awake	children	diaries	fried
baby	chin	diary	frighten
back	chop	dinner	fringe
bake	click	dive	frock
baker	cliff	doing	frog
balloon	clip	door	frost
band	clock	doze	frying
bank	clog	dozing	funny
bark	club	dress	gas
bee	coached	drive	gate
bill	cobbler	driver	girl
bird	cold	dry	gladiator
black	colder	duck	glare
bleed	come	duckling	glitter
blind	coming	dummy	gloss
block	cone	dune	glow
blow	core	each	going
blunt	corn	ear	goldfish
body	corner	editor	grab
bonfire	cost	eye	grand
boring	count	eyebrows	grandfather
born	cowboy	eyes	grass
both	crab	face	gravy
brake	crack	fair	greenhouse
brave	cracker	fairies	grin
brick	crane	fairy	grinned
bride	crawl	fake	groom
brook	crayons	fast	grow
brother	creak	father	grunt

52 © 2005 Stephen Curran

Book Two Word List

guitar	late	oar	rang
hair	law	oilcan	rent
hall	left	one	rise
handbag	lesson	only	river
handlebars	letter	other	rock
handpump	lick	over	rockery
hang	lied	pace	roof
happy	life	pack	rook
hard	lift	pain	rose
hate	list	paint	rotor
hawk	little	painting	rubbing
hear	lock	park	rule
heather	lollies	pebble	rush
held	love	pedal	safe
herself	loving	penny	sake
himself	lump	pick	sang
home	lure	pile	save
hood	lute	pillar box	scold
hook	making	pine	scratches
hoped	male	pinned	seat
horn	mark	place	seaweed
horse	market	plan	seed
house	mate	plant	seem
hunt	meet	plate	seven
hunter	meteor	plum	sheet
hurries	mind	poise	shell
hutch	miss	poking	shelves
itches	mist	policeman	shine
itself	more	pond	shot
jaw	most	poor	shovel
joking	moth	post	show
joy	mother	pretty	sick
just	mouse	prickle	sideboard
kerb	mouth	prune	sister
kick	mucky	pruning	skater
kind	mudguard	pump	ski
kiss	mule	purrs	skid
kite	mummy	push	skin
kitten	mute	queen	skin diver
lace	myself	quick	skinny
lady	named	race	skylark
lake	near	rain	slack
lamp	neck	raining	slam
last	nose	rake	slammed

© 2005 Stephen Curran

Book Two Word List

slap	stick	teach	wake
slate	sticker	teacher	walk
sleep	sting	teapot	water
sleeping	stoat	tee shirt	wave
slide	stood	than	wax
slime	store	thank	weed
slot	storing	thick	week
slug	storm	thinner	west
slush	story	three	whale
smell	strap	thump	wheelbarrow
smile	street	tick	while
smoke	strict	ticket	whinny
snap	string	toddler	whirl
snow	stump	toffee	whisk
sold	summer	tone	wide
son	sundial	trace	width
sorry	sunflowers	trail	wife
spanner	sunny	train	wild
spend	supper	trainers	wind
spent	surprise	trick	wing
spin	swell	trowel	winner
spoke	swim	tubing	winning
spoon	swing	tummy	winter
staff	table	tuning	wobble
stall	tail	tyre	wolves
stamp	talk	wait	worried
stem	tea	waiting	year

Congratulations!

You have now learnt to spell **920** words; know what they mean and how to use them in a sentence.

Now move on to **Book 3** to learn lots more words to add to your word bank total.

Answers

Key Stage 2 Spelling & Vocabulary Workbook 2

Exercise 24a
1) raining
2) hall
3) count
4) mother
5) other
6) nose
7) going
8) Father
9) mouth
10) train

Exercise 24b
11) doing
12) rose
13) find
14) found
15) again
16) home
17) brother
18) wind
19) kind
20) rain

Crossword No. 24

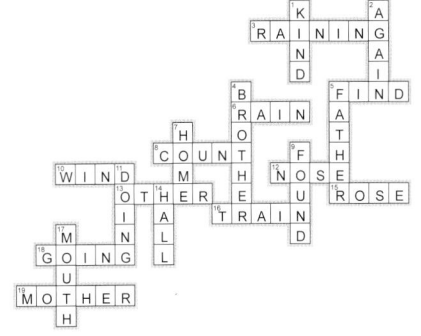

Letter = O

Exercise 25a
1) able
2) duck
3) water
4) dinner
5) fly
6) late
7) seven
8) butter
9) winter
10) dry

Exercise 25b
11) supper
12) Black
13) bill
14) ate
15) table
16) back
17) summer
18) gate
19) sick
20) sister

Crossword No. 25

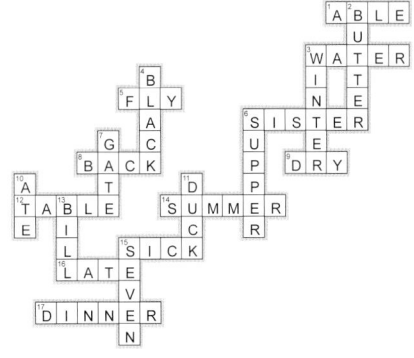

Letter = L

Exercise 26a
1) show
2) girl
3) arm
4) love
5) lesson
6) happy
7) kitten
8) letter
9) dark
10) grow

Exercise 26b
11) first
12) snow
13) sunny
14) hard
15) sorry
16) funny
17) one
18) bird
19) little
20) Blow

Crossword No. 26

Letter = O

Key Stage 2 Spelling & Vocabulary Workbook 2

Answers

Exercise 27a
1) story
2) hair
3) baby
4) each
5) river
6) sold
7) Come
8) smoke
9) spoke
10) fire

Exercise 27b
11) grass
12) fast
13) chair
14) last
15) making
16) coming
17) fairy
18) dress
19) pretty
20) fair

Exercise 28a
1) cold
2) near
3) house
4) hear
5) ask
6) over
7) add
8) walk
9) horse
10) year

Exercise 28b
11) only
12) mouse
13) colder
14) than
15) penny
16) talk
17) dear
18) apple
19) after
20) ear

Exercise 29a
1) rent
2) lady
3) swing
4) damp
5) camp
6) tail
7) spend
8) wing
9) store
10) eyes

Exercise 29b
11) left
12) face
13) plant
14) spent
15) Wait
16) race
17) lamp
18) more
19) eye
20) miss

Crossword No. 27

Crossword No. 28

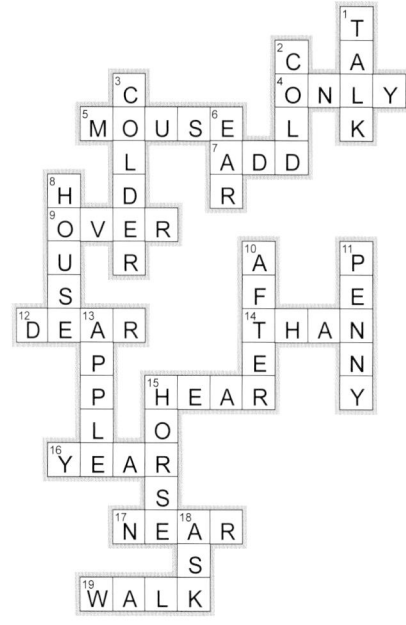

Crossword No. 29

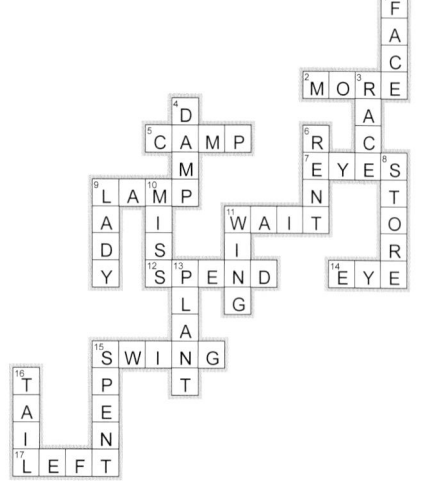

Letter = A

Letter = F

Letter = L

© 2005 Stephen Curran

Answers

Key Stage 2 Spelling & Vocabulary Workbook 2

Exercise 30a
1) plum
2) Rock
3) block
4) spin
5) lump
6) hang
7) west
8) stick
9) blunt
10) weed

Exercise 30b
11) string
12) clock
13) sting
14) seed
15) plan
16) pump
17) bleed
18) stamp
19) lock
20) skin

Exercise 31a
1) rush
2) shot
3) pack
4) sang
5) rang
6) fond
7) seem
8) pond
9) crack
10) thank

Exercise 31b
11) band
12) chin
13) pick
14) bank
15) chop
16) brick
17) Just
18) crush
19) trick
20) brush

Exercise 32a
1) stood
2) driver
3) crane
4) club
5) hunt
6) lake
7) bake
8) smell
9) cave
10) wave

Exercise 32b
11) safe
12) brave
13) shell
14) hunter
15) save
16) hook
17) swell
18) drive
19) dive
20) hood

Crossword No. 30

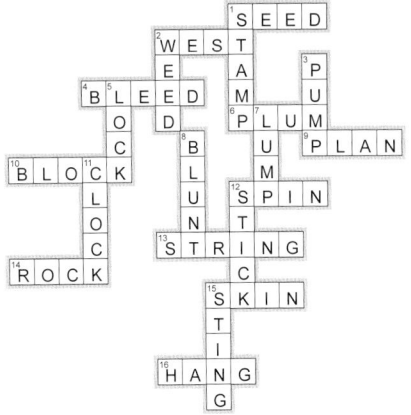

Letter = T

Crossword No. 31

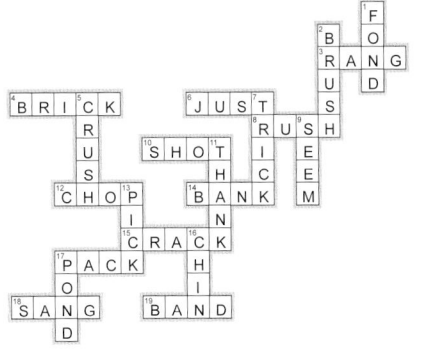

Letter = B

Crossword No. 32

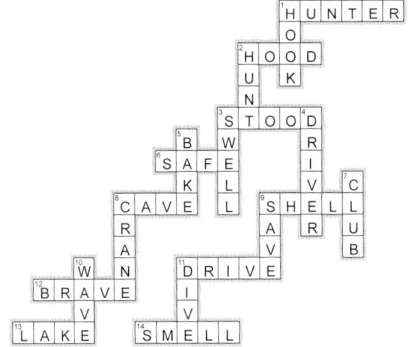

Letter = A

At the Zoo
1. SIGNPOST
2. RHINOCEROS
3. ENTRANCE
4. PARROT
5. TYRE
6. KANGAROO
7. GIRAFFE
8. TIGER
9. BROOM
10. ROPE
11. CAMEL
12. LIONS
13. POLAR BEAR
14. ZOO KEEPER
15. GORILLA

On the Farm
1. TROUGH
2. CHICKEN
3. FENCE
4. BOOT
5. PITCHFORK
6. BARN
7. SHEEPDOG
8. FARMER
9. PIGLET
10. CART
11. CROW
12. FARMHOUSE
13. GOAT
14. CHURN
15. TRACTOR

© 2005 Stephen Curran

Key Stage 2 Spelling & Vocabulary Workbook 2

Answers

Exercise 33a
1) bee
2) *Three*
3) plate
4) baker
5) date
6) sheet
7) street
8) awake
9) named
10) hate

Exercise 33b
11) rise
12) week
13) sake
14) mist
15) spoon
16) list
17) lift
18) wake
19) meet
20) rake

Crossword No. 33

Letter = E

Exercise 34a
1) queen
2) painting
3) chase
4) while
5) chain
6) asleep
7) pile
8) pine
9) pain
10) shine

Exercise 34b
11) free
12) fine
13) mate
14) case
15) paint
16) Creep
17) sleeping
18) sleep
19) waiting
20) smile

Crossword No. 34

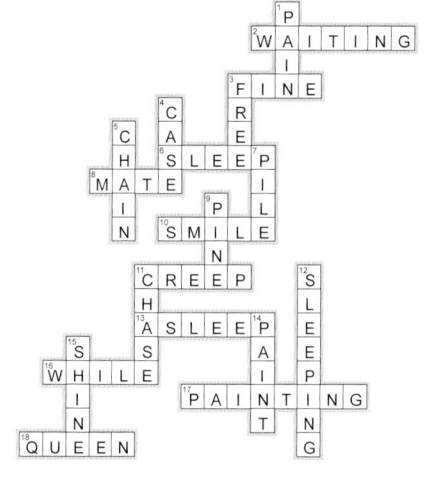

Letter = H

Exercise 35a
1) grandfather
2) herself
3) cost
4) slide
5) push
6) moth
7) wife
8) son
9) wide
10) hoped

Exercise 35b
11) myself
12) bush
13) himself
14) stem
15) frost
16) grand
17) life
18) place
19) frog
20) lace

Crossword No. 35

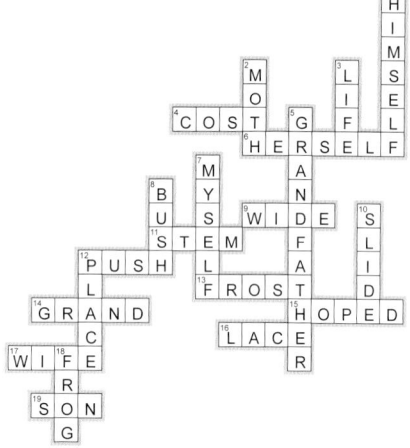

Letter = R

© 2005 Stephen Curran

Answers

Key Stage 2 Spelling & Vocabulary Workbook 2

Exercise 36a
1) itself
2) strap
3) children
4) horn
5) blind
6) held
7) thick
8) kick
9) wild
10) neck

Exercise 36b
11) kiss
12) another
13) body
14) child
15) both
16) fold
17) scold
18) lick
19) mind
20) snap

Exercise 37a
1) corner
2) born
3) ticket
4) swim
5) teacher
6) market
7) park
8) corn
9) stump
10) post

Exercise 37b
11) bark
12) gas
13) crab
14) storm
15) teach
16) quick
17) most
18) mark
19) joy
20) tea

Exercise 38a
1) poor
2) boring
3) poking
4) staff
5) roof
6) loving
7) pruning
8) curing
9) dozing
10) door

Exercise 38b
11) tubing
12) cracker
13) tuning
14) balloon
15) doze
16) toffee
17) joking
18) prune
19) floor
20) storing

Crossword No. 36

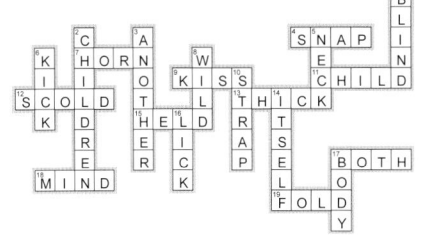

Crossword No. 37

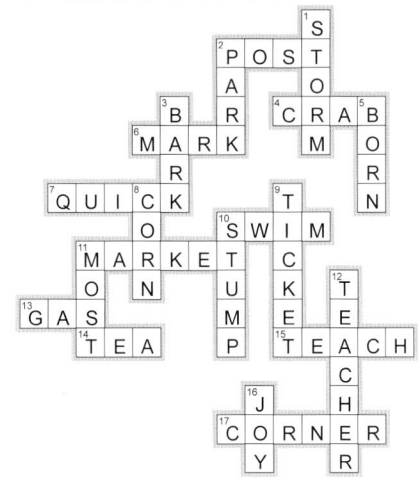

Crossword No. 38

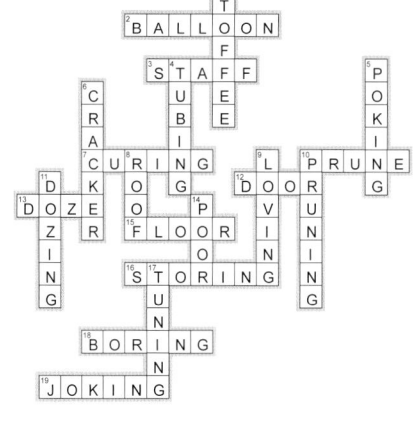

Letter = C

Letter = T

Letter = E

At the Airport
1. LOUDSPEAKER
2. WING
3. DUTY-FREE
4. PASSPORT
5. LITTER BIN
6. CHECK-IN
7. RUCKSACK
8. LABEL
9. BRIEFCASE
10. AEROPLANE
11. TICKET
12. AIRCREW
13. RADAR
14. TROLLEY
15. GIRDERS

At the Port
1. CRANE
2. RAMP
3. JETTY
4. SAILOR
5. CRATE
6. FLAG
7. BUOY
8. PORTHOLES
9. SEAGULL
10. WARSHIP
11. HOVERCRAFT
12. ANCHOR
13. CABLE
14. FUNNEL
15. MAST

© 2005 Stephen Curran

Key Stage 2 Spelling & Vocabulary Workbook 2

Answers

Exercise 39a
1) sideboard
2) diaries
3) slammed
4) tyre
5) thinner
6) hawk
7) law
8) stall
9) lollies
10) tummy

Exercise 39b
11) mummy
12) mudguard
13) fairies
14) pinned
15) grinned
16) winning
17) diary
18) dummy
19) jaw
20) winner

Crossword No. 39

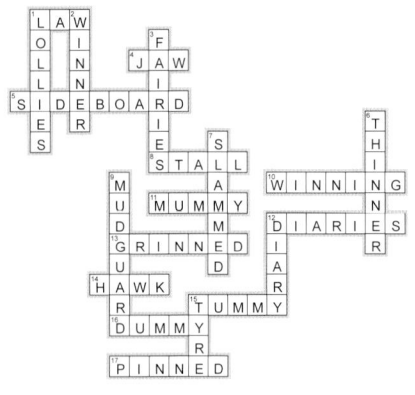

Letter = M

Exercise 40a
1) goldfish
2) lied
3) cobbler
4) oilcan
5) wobble
6) handpump
7) pebble
8) foxes
9) fried
10) wax

Exercise 40b
11) rubbing
12) handlebars
13) canary
14) spanner
15) pace
16) prickle
17) trace
18) bubble
19) freckle
20) pedal

Crossword No. 40

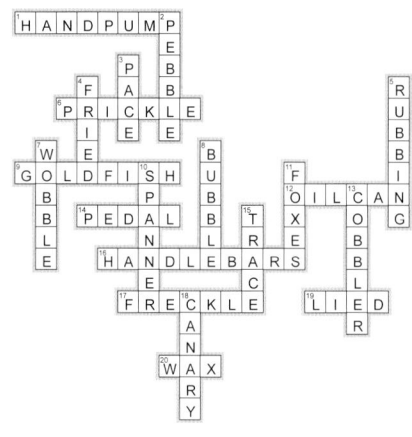

Letter = E

Exercise 41a
1) whale
2) shelves
3) policeman
4) budgerigar
5) eyebrows
6) aircraft
7) curved
8) shovel
9) frying
10) calves

Exercise 41b
11) Wolves
12) toddler
13) pillar box
14) guitar
15) kerb
16) assistant
17) seaweed
18) surprise
19) strict
20) handbag

Crossword No. 41

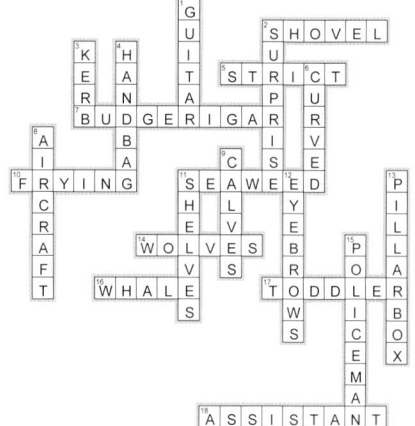

Letter = E

© 2005 Stephen Curran

Answers

Key Stage 2 Spelling & Vocabulary Workbook 2

Exercise 42a
1) itches
2) rotor
3) sunflowers
4) thump
5) heather
6) meteor
7) anchor
8) greenhouse
9) wheelbarrow
10) Bonfire

Exercise 42b
11) scratches
12) editor
13) crook
14) purrs
15) worried
16) hutch
17) hurries
18) rockery
19) sundial
20) trowel

Exercise 43a
1) crayons
2) tee shirt
3) clog
4) glitter
5) brook
6) crop
7) bride
8) Cast
9) crawl
10) glow

Exercise 43b
11) creak
12) rook
13) crocodile
14) brake
15) crisps
16) clip
17) cliff
18) width
19) tick
20) click

Exercise 44a
1) skinny
2) skin diver
3) freezer
4) fridge
5) ski
6) gladiator
7) grin
8) frighten
9) frock
10) fringe

Exercise 44b
11) skater
12) trail
13) skid
14) trainers
15) grab
16) glare
17) gravy
18) gloss
19) groom
20) grunt

Crossword No. 42

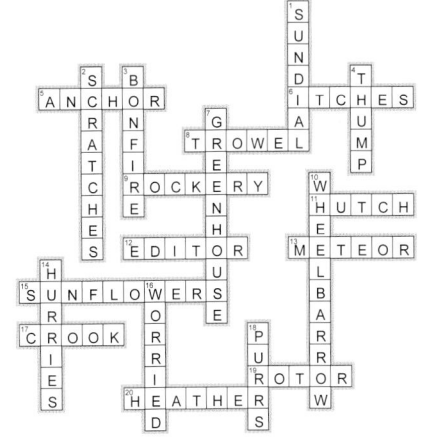

Crossword No. 43

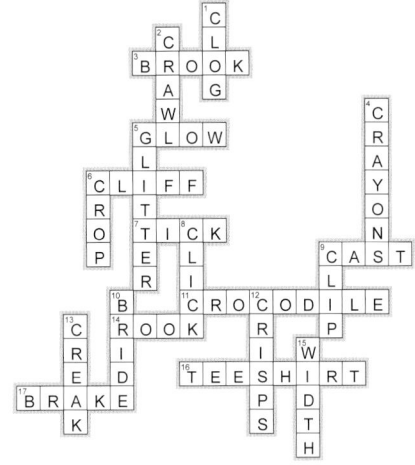

Crossword No. 44

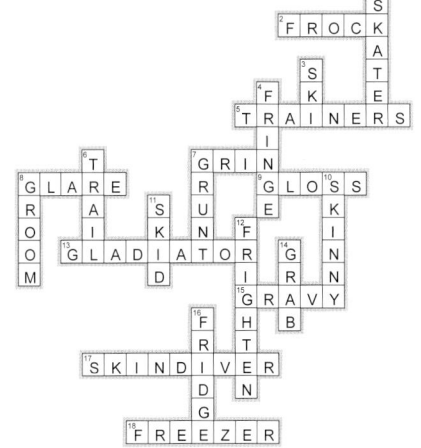

Letter = C

Letter = I

Letter = R

© 2005 Stephen Curran

Key Stage 2 Spelling & Vocabulary Workbook 2

Answers

Exercise 45a
1) skylark
2) coached
3) whinny
4) slot
5) slate
6) seat
7) oar
8) slime
9) whisk
10) teapot

Exercise 45b
11) slack
12) slush
13) slug
14) slap
15) curly
16) cowboy
17) foil
18) Curry
19) slam
20) whirl

Crossword No. 45

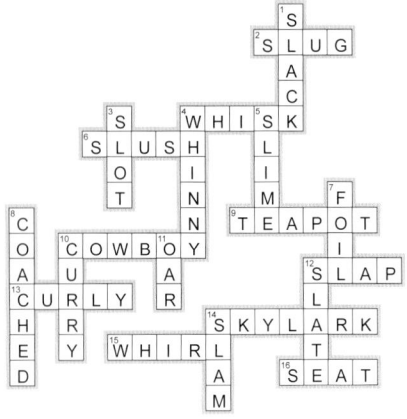

Letter = A

Exercise 46a
1) lure
2) stoat
3) duckling
4) poise
5) lute
6) anywhere
7) tone
8) mute
9) sticker
10) anyone

Exercise 46b
11) cube
12) fake
13) core
14) mucky
15) dune
16) rule
17) kite
18) male
19) mule
20) cone

Crossword No. 46

Letter = C

Mystery Word
O L O A F L T B
F O O T B A L L

Mystery Word
A E H R C T E
T E A C H E R

Mystery Word
M E E C I R A C
I C E C R E A M

PROGRESS CHARTS

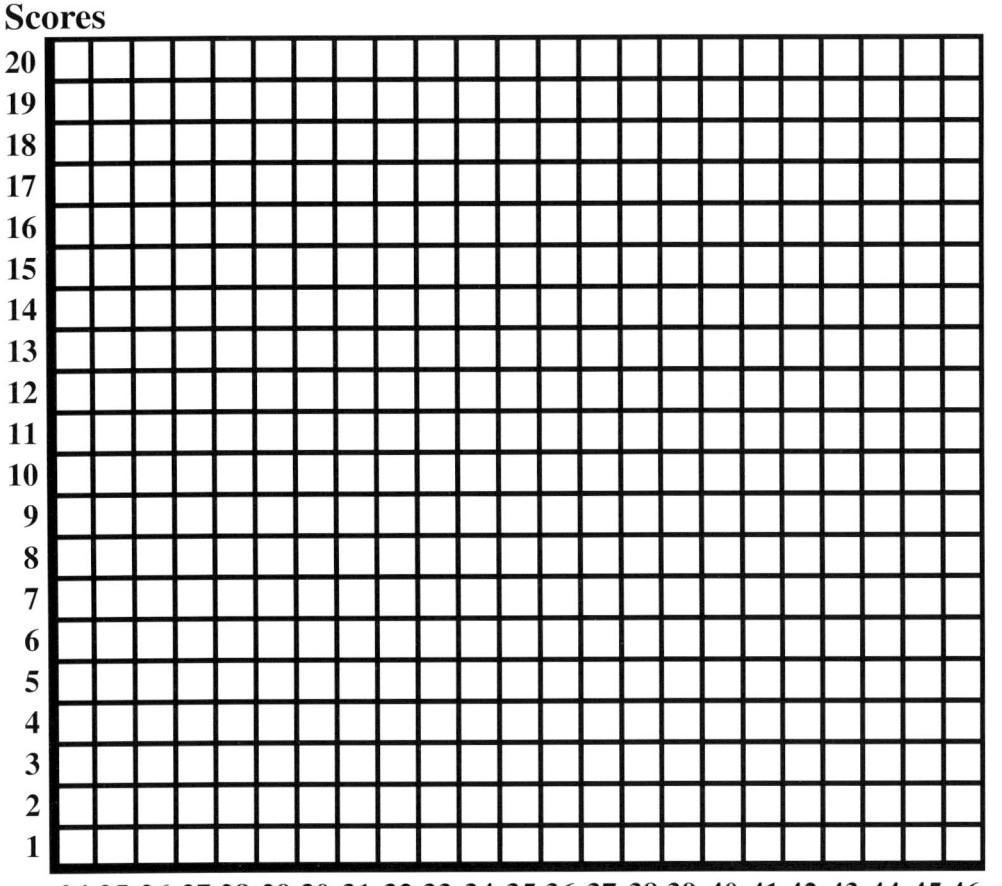

Exercises

Shade in your score for each exercise on the graph. Add them up for your total score out of 460. Ask an adult to work out the percentage.

Total Score

Percentage

 A

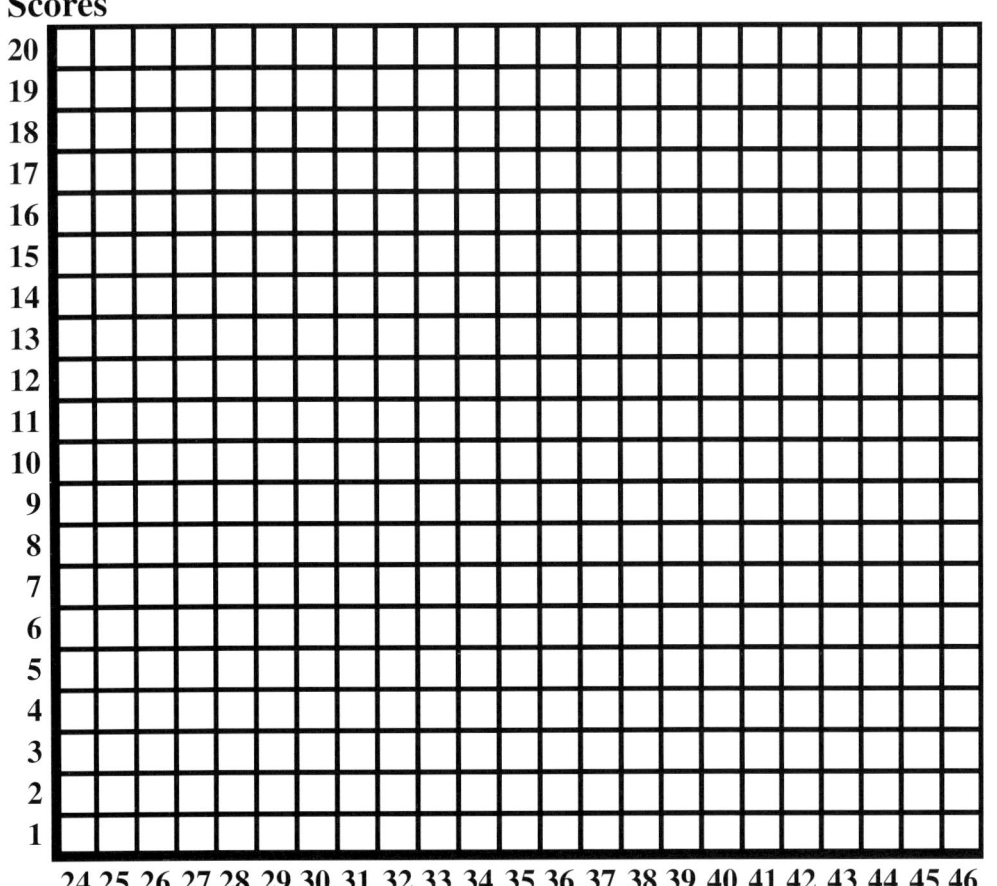

Crosswords

Shade in your score for each crossword on the graph. Add them up for your total score out of 460.

Total Score

Percentage

 B

For the average percentage add %A and %B and divide by 2

Overall Percentage

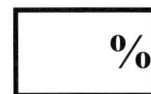

© 2005 Stephen Curran

CERTIFICATE OF ACHIEVEMENT

This certifies

_____

has successfully completed

Key Stage 2
Spelling & Vocabulary
WORKBOOK 2

Overall percentage score achieved [   ] %

Comment _____
_____

Signed _____
(teacher/parent/guardian)

Date _____